Bruce E. Massis, MLS, MA

The Challenges to Library Learning
Solutions for Librarians

The Challenges to Library Learning

Solutions for Librarians

Routledge Studies in Library and Information Science

The Challenges to Library Learning
Solutions for Librarians

Bruce E. Massis, MLS, MA

Routledge
Taylor & Francis Group

NEW YORK AND LONDON

First published 2008
by Routledge
270 Madison Ave, New York, NY 10016

Simultaneously published in the UK
by Routledge
2 Park Square, Milton Park, Abingdon, Oxon OX14 4RN

Routledge is an imprint of the Taylor & Francis Group, an informa business

© 2008 Taylor & Francis

Printed and bound in the United States of America on acid-free paper by
Edwards Brothers Digital Book Center

Library of Congress Cataloging in Publication Data
    The challenges to library learning {:} solutions for librarians / Bruce E.
Massis.
        p. cm.
    Includes bibliographical references.
    1. Library employees—In-service training. 2. Librarians—In-service
training. 3. Library
    education (Continuing education) 4. Library personnel management. 5.
Employee motivation. I. Massis, Bruce E.
    Z668.5.C47 2007
    023'.8—dc22
                                                                    2007039819

ISBN 10: 0-7890-3141-8 (hbk)
ISBN 10: 0-2038-8939-8 (ebk)

ISBN 13: 978-0-7890-3141-9 (hbk)
ISBN 13: 978-0-2038-8939-8 (ebk)

A library is the best possible imitation, by human beings, of a divine mind . . . we have invented libraries because we know that we do not have divine powers, but we try to do our best to imitate them.

Umberto Eco

Consequently, simply asking questions about the future of libraries, let alone working to transform them for the digital age, almost inevitably evokes anguished, poignant, and even hostile responses filled with nostalgia for a near-mythical institution.

Anonymous

So what, exactly, do you people do here?

Traci Aquara

ABOUT THE AUTHOR

Bruce E. Massis, MLS, MA, is Director of the Educational Resources Center at Columbus State Community College in Columbus, Ohio. He has served as a library administrator in multitype library consortia (SEFLIN, SCLS), public (Brooklyn and Hoboken Public Libraries), special (JGB Cassette Library International), and academic libraries (Adelphi University and CSCC) for more than three decades. Mr. Massis has worked in an official capacity within the International Federation of Library Associations (IFLA) and spent more than 20 years cooperatively developing programs, projects, and policies with international library colleagues. Active in numerous library associations and widely published, his books include *Interlibrary Loan of Alternative Format Materials; The Practical Library Manager; The Practical Library Trainer* (all from Haworth); *Serving Print Disabled Library Patrons; Library Service for the Blind and Physically Handicapped: An International Approach;* and *Models of Cooperation in the US, Latin America, and Caribbean Libraries.*

CONTENTS

Acknowledgments

I am particularly indebted to the team at SEFLIN for their overwhelming friendship and support and, specifically, Executive Director Tom Sloan, who guided and supported my work in service to the member libraries. Also, thanks to my friends and colleagues in the *Learning Futures Forum* whose collective brilliance inspires me as a librarian and educator. Finally, I would like to acknowledge my mom and dad, especially my mom who reminded me never to lose my curiosity.

Introduction

There are a number of challenges to lifelong learning that confront library staff today. Library staff continue to endure staff shortages, depleted or eliminated budget lines for continuous education, longer library operating hours, increased workloads, more demands by the public, scheduled and unscheduled technology upgrades, and simply the widespread atmosphere in libraries today of relentless change.

Still, any challenge can be surmounted if there is an understandable and clearly communicated discussion and suggested solution in order to overcome the obstacles. So, what better rationale for being engaged in a program of lifelong learning than with the goal of substantially and continually upgrading one's skills in order to remain actively engaged in the workplace?

Technology has impacted libraries to the point where many of today's students view the library as more than a convenient place to study; it is a necessary tool in their arsenal of other learning tools in order to ensure success. Students accept multitasking as the norm. They enter the library, not only seeking a quiet refuge to study using their wireless laptops, but during a study session may also utilize a full range of technological communication devices to complete their study session, including speaking on their cell phones, listening to their MP3 players, and instant messaging their friends at 100 words per minute. With all that activity occurring concurrently, they may still walk up to the reference desk to have their reference question answered. Is the library staff ready to attend to this student in the same vein in which they work? Are they engaged in this perpetual flow as the student? In order to be engaged in lifelong learning, one must first be engaged in the workplace itself, and one must remain engaged. A higher level of engagement in the workplace can be an outcome of lifelong learning. Library staff must then be proactive in seeking out opportunities for engagement, not only with their customers, but also within themselves.

There is risk in administrators providing leadership to staff who have not remained engaged in the workplace, and thus have their visions for service fall on deaf ears. Individuals can exist on a level of apathy or exhibit a laissez faire attitude that can be demonstrated as an unwillingness to learn something, anything new. Can such indifference be countered with an inclusive program of continuous learning that seeks to fully engage all staff? If offered, will staff avail themselves of the learning opportunities?

There is a dual responsibility inherent in adult education. There is the responsibility of the library administrator to make available learning opportunities that are not only continuous, but are also both general and job specific. However, there is also the responsibility of the library staff, recognizing the value of continuous education, to take advantage of these offerings.

What are the rewards? These can be many, both financial and nonfinancial. The financial benefits may be seen in salary increases that may accompany increased knowledge-based skills. More often, however, the rewards are those that benefit the employee, if not monetarily, at least psychologically and practically. One's self-confidence can always benefit from the recognition of support from one's superiors and/or the profession itself.

What value-added strategies can be employed by managers to create a system of nonmonetary rewards in order to support lifelong learning in libraries and, therefore, increased staff engagement? If so, what are the proper rewards to the successful completion of a course, a workshop, a Webinar, or in its extreme, an advanced or additional degree?

This book strives to delineate and define certain challenges that impede lifelong learning for library staff today. There are also suggestions offered, where possible, to meet and/or defeat those challenges while empowering the individual adult learner to benefit from a goal-oriented approach to learning that goes beyond the "what's in it for me" scenario. After all, what could be more rewarding than overcoming a challenge and succeeding in meeting a goal one has set for oneself.

The sustainability of continuing education and training lies in the concept that learning is not an isolated experience, but that it is viewed as an integral part of every staff members' responsibility.

To support this commitment, the library must seek to create a "blended learning" program for staff and a fully interactive presence that would fill the need to transform the library learning culture into a "Community of Learning." A portion of this book concentrates on the creation and philosophy of this Community of Learning concept wherein the focus is jointly placed on both the institution and the individual to actively perform in an atmosphere of continuous learning. The goal of the program was to make available numerous learning opportunities for library staff in order to remain engaged and well trained.

The concept of the continuous learning program for library staff being developed in order to provide lifelong learning opportunities for library staff is becoming standard practice in many libraries and library-support organizations, such as library consortia or library cooperatives. In fact, today, the primary service deliverable in many library cooperatives is continuing education. There is recognition of this by state libraries around the country resulting in annual Library Services and Technology Act (LSTA) grant funding for either competitive or noncompetitive continuing education programs.

If adult learning offers anything, it is a reiteration of the *can do* philosophy that excited us so much as students in our grade-school days. Such enthusiasm for learning is a light that should never be dimmed. In the workplace, however, it must be a cooperative venture between employer and employee to make it successful. A learning system, once in place, must be supported by the library and maintained by an intellectually engaged staff. After all, one must never lose one's intellectual curiosity. In retaining that curiosity, the library learner may well enhance his or her engagement in the workplace. Study, itself, in the form of lifelong learning, should afford the learner engagement enough in the workplace. However, does it, and what are the challenges to the process? In this work, I respond to this question with several solutions.

Chapter 1

The Rules of Engagement

The Challenge—Overcoming Staff Disengagement

At some point, every employee must ask himself or herself whether he or she is simply *busy* or *actively engaged.* The online environment has placed so many distractions in our path to productivity that it is easier now than ever to succumb to distractions throughout the work-day. All of us will readily admit to being *busy* in the workplace, but is there something within us where the spark of curiosity and the need for continuous learning still burns? Although the issues of recruitment and retention are certainly linked to staff engagement, what about the strategy of continuous learning as a means to achieve a level of staff engagement as well? Is the connection between being actively engaged on the job and engaged in continuous learning connected so that should a program of continuous learning made available to staff, would that alone be enough to keep employees actively engaged?

Studies have indicated that only one-quarter of the workforce is actively engaged in the workplace. There has even been a best seller in France titled, *Bonjour Paresse,* a work whose title literally trans-lates as "Hello Laziness," the subtitle of which reads "The Art and the Importance of Doing the Least Possible in the Workplace." The author is Corinne Maier, who has become a popular figure almost overnight by encouraging the country's workers to adopt her strategy of "active disengagement" and "premeditated idleness" to escape the daily grind. As cynical as this approach may be, there is a reason why it has become the best seller that it has. The book has touched a nerve, and as frightening as it may be to managers and administrators, given the numbers of employees entering the ranks of the disengaged, the issue must be addressed.

In Italy, there has even been a "conference of the lazy," which may or may not be different from active disengagement. The conference held workshops addressing both sides of the issue, from the management as well as the employee perspective. So, what is going on here? Has the time come for a reevaluation of the workforce in every organization in order to determine not necessarily the level of engagement, but the level of disengagement? When the bottom line reflects this trend in the corporate sector, actions can be taken. When it occurs in the nonprofit or public sector, what can be done? What actions are practicable?

If large numbers of employees, many of whom are seated in front of their workstations for most of everyday, are surfing the Web, shopping, organizing their vacation plans, logging onto the personal video Web sites, chatting, and the like, what steps can be taken to curtail these activities and reengage them in the work of the organization? Does disengagement in the workplace lead to engaging in these activities out of boredom, lack of direction, lax or little management oversight, then, there are obviously greater issues that need to be addressed within the organization.

If the level of disengagement is as widespread as is reported, then the effect can certainly be felt on the bottom line. If there was any question as to whether or not there is a bottom line, make no mistake about it—there is a bottom line in every library's budget. It may not be visible to those who entered library work expecting it to be the model of the "service" industry, where the only real bottom line has more to do with issues unrelated to finance, but more related to service. However, there is very much a bottom line. Just ask any library director, board trustee, or CFO.

In fact, a Gallup study reveals that "the ratio of engaged to disengaged workers drives the financial outcomes of any organization. More than 42 independent Gallup studies indicate that only one in four employees is engaged at work. A full 75 percent of the workforce of most companies is not fully engaged on the job."[1]

One in four! What ought to be management's response to this astonishing figure: to throw up one's collective hands? Or is it time to examine measures that must be taken to reengage these employees, and if so, to what level can they be brought back? What are some suggested strategies related to lifelong learning in libraries that can serve to narrow this *engagement gap* and breathe life into library employees whose sense of engagement has waned? How can managers help their library staff remain actively engaged in the workplace and continue to learn, not only through guidance and motivation, but also through a learning program of self-directed initiatives.

One response could be "incentives." In libraries, the program of rewards for staff has not been as robust as it could be. Often, of course, this may have less to do with the will to do so than with limited funding. This is always an issue, and library administrators spend a great deal of time seeking a balance between salaries and service with the limited funds available. However, this decision can also be made using the rationale that since the staff is the library's most-valued resource, there must be a greater effort to augment their knowledge base and skill level on the job. Perhaps libraries must begin to offer greater rewards for those who exhibit and succeed in active engagement in the program of lifelong learning. Rewards can easily be offered for the completion of courses or workshops available through an annual staff training program.

If lifelong learning is promoted and supported as a value-added incentive, the program can serve as a positive response and reinforcement to staff that have become disengaged. A comprehensive blended learning program, offering a wide variety of training workshops, tutorials, and classes can conceivably serve as a spark of inspiration for those staff seeking greater fulfillment on the job. Then, upon completion of this added incentive and armed with their new skills, employees can find renewed meaning in their present positions and perhaps even strive for higher or more diverse positions in their organization.

There is a great deal of commonality between employees in the private sector and those who work in our libraries. In many staff satisfaction surveys, response data indicates that financial rewards do not tend to be the primary drivers behind satisfaction and engagement in the workplace. There are a number of other factors identified by respondents as more important than salary that determine employee fulfillment in the workplace. Benefits, flex-time, childcare, supervisor respect, and, of course, educational opportunities (certificate, non-degree, degree, and continuing education) have all been identified as greater determining factors in job satisfaction than salary. Realistically, given the annual increases in employee health insurance, about the only benefit the annual single-digit salary increase is likely to cover is the double-digit health insurance increase.

The supervisor's attitude and knowledge about learning has a tremendous impact on the development of employees. Also, the creation of the workplace as a learning place is a strategy that may be successfully employed, that is creating an environment where the climate of continuous learning is not only developed, but wherein the learning is tagged to upgrading skills to remain at the same (or hopefully higher) level than the library patron, with the goal of providing an enhanced level of customer service. Building the knowledge base of the employee is empowering and can provide the employee with a greater level of confidence through shared awareness and practice.

Thomas D. Fisher, writing in *Self-Directedness in the Workplace: A Re-Examination,* also suggests turning the workplace into a classroom. Fisher writes of the "learning contract" where both the manager and the employee understand the shared responsibility of the learning experience in the workplace. This can be accomplished with the creation of a "field of practice" developed by library managers with the goal of providing a place and time for staff to learn in a quiet, private environment without interruption. If each "field of practice" can be developed and supported, then, learning objectives and expectations can be specifically and personally designed for each individual employee. This can be done at the annual and/or semiannual staff performance evaluation meeting. The staffer can discuss and understand the expectations, and the manager can indicate that accomplishments and that which has not be accomplished will be further discussed with the employee at the six-month and annual performance evaluation meeting with the employee. What is even more important in this scenario is the employee's opportunity to indicate not only what *has* been accomplished in his or her "field of practice" during the first and second performance evaluations, but also what *has not* been accomplished. This discussion during the performance evaluation is very important because it provides the employee with the platform to work with the manager to either redesign expectations or realign them to meet the appropriate set of goals expectations. It then becomes the responsibility of the learner to use the opportunity that he or she has been given for learning.

Given the nature of staffing in libraries, it is often difficult to create such a concept. Due to the usual issue of short staffing and/or tight budgets, this may only be possible where there is agreement by the employee that the "field of practice" can only be established after the employee leaves the workplace and returns home. If this is the case, there may be an opportunity to offer the employee a financial or other tangible incentive to complete this training at home. Still, if it is possible to create this in the workplace and provide time and space for it to happen, there can be greater buy-in by the employee, resulting in an enhanced level of loyalty and trust between employee and employer.

While engaged in learning using this strategy, a bond between employer and employee can develop through a trust that can be built through the employer who trusts that the employee will become engaged in learning and that the employee will be granted the time and place in which to indulge in this practice. The self-directed nature of this method of learning falls to the learner, and on the other hand, if the learner chooses not to take the time, and *not* learn, the "learning contract" within the field of practice has been violated and the learner's disengagement has won the day.

Rather than individual learning, the library may seek to create a group learning environment. Should the learner feel that he or she would be more productive in a group learning environment, Fisher suggests the establishment of what he terms, "study circles." In such an environment, the level of engagement may be heightened through the support mechanism within the group learning structure. Employees engaged in study circles may find greater rewards than learning on their own simply because most of us have come through the standard practice of classroom education and many are used to the concept of a "study circle." In such an atmosphere, there is often greater pressure to succeed, especially when all members of the circle are required to produce in order to succeed. If the level of engagement among members starts to dissipate, it is up to the study circle's members to energize the group. How do study circles (i.e., learning teams) support learning in this environment?

According to the Virtual Teacher Center in the United Kingdom, "[t]he team approach provides safety for participants so that they feel comfortable sharing ideas. It also encourages better situational analysis and provides for opportunities to generate new and innovative ideas. Workload can be shared thereby enabling a complex task to be completed more efficiently."[2]

Mary Grassinger, project manager for SMDC Health Systems, emphasizes that to retain a sense of engagement means to uphold a positive attitude in the workplace.

Managing disengaged employees is a chore that requires an infinite amount of work that may yield little or no results. Managing engaged employees, however, can be an absolute joy and a pleasure. The shared sense of excitement and experience can fuel the individual and the team to greater and more prolonged successes. Using the suggestions in this chapter can assist the manager in properly leading their staff into reigniting their engagement.

If, as an individual, one feels a sense of disengagement, one must ask whether the problem lies within one's self, the organization, or both. We can seek to initiate change in ourselves. Regarding change in the workplace, however, one may have little or no power to effect such change. If one does, however, each individual must strive to contribute in order to add value to the workplace. If not, and the workplace environment is such that full engagement is either discouraged or ignored, then one must take responsibility for one's own success or lack thereof.

Likewise, it is the responsibility of the organization to establish the concept of employee engagement as the centerpiece of a positive and productive workplace environment. Iain Parsons of Best Companies suggests that "employee engagement needed to be part of the mix all the way through." He also said, "Organisations that take the time, will undoubtedly improve workplace engagement, and resultantly the motivation and performance of their people. There had to be a focus on developing individuals and establishing clear communication flows."[3]

Parsons touches on the most important element in organizations for those who wish to be successful in engaging their employees, that of "communication." However, for successful communication to be present, there must be a willingness by both the organization and the employee to communicate clearly.

The classic communications model indicates that the following components must be in place for successful communication to occur. These components are

- the sender
- the message
- the channel
- the receiver
- feedback
- context.

If any one of these components is disturbed by what has become an environment described in a report issued by the American Society for Training and Development (ASTD) as "disruptive change," several of those components can become corrupted and successful communication cannot be achieved.

The challenge to lifelong learning for library staff discussed in this chapter is lack of employee engagement. Because we currently spend 70 to 80 percent of our workday communicating, whether it is virtual, face to face, writing, faxing, e-mail, and the like, by percentage, it is the one most important aspect of our workplace engagements that both the organization and the individual must become experts in to be successful.

In conclusion, the library must first recognize the level of engagement of its employees; if that analysis yields information resulting in an unsatisfactory result, then, that must be communicated to the employees along with a designated plan to address the issue. The plan must include a program of lifelong learning opportunities, a field of practice, recognition and rewards for success, positive impact on the annual personnel review, and constant communication between the library and the staff including all of the components of the communication loop.

Chapter 2

E-Learning for Library Staff

The Challenge—Accepting E-Learning As a Routine Learning Model

When the mission statement of The Boston Center for Adult Education was developed in 1933, the aim was to create an environment where "small groups of men and women would meet together in living room settings to learn, discuss, and create for the sheer pleasure of doing so."[1] Surprising as it may appear to those who have not indulged in the e-learning arena is that a similar environment can also be created despite the physical presence of either the instructor or the class.

When adult students enter the online learning environment, many are not exactly certain what to expect. In a comprehensive "blended learning" program where e-learning is incorporated into a fully functional package of live instruction, teleconferences, Web delivery of content, and the like, the opportunity to learn in this "anywhere, anytime" environment can become an attractive and valued learning tool. However, it can also present certain challenges unique to the online learning environment.

It is quite clear that all libraries are increasing their dependency upon technology as a means by which the communication of information and the importance of information literacy is transferred to its users. Some library staff continue to experience an increased level of anxiety because of the constant changes and added pressures that come along with such dependency. This is often attributable to perception that the public has yet to fully comprehend that there are numerous and valid information resources that are nontechnologically driven. There is a public expectation of a high level of technical expertise among library staff. However, it is equally clear that the public has not accepted the notion that there remain other avenues of approach when seeking information. That has certainly been a challenge to the reference librarian, who, when conducting the reference interview with a patron expects his or her suggested resource to be an electronic one, may still receive an answer using a better and more trusted *print* resource. The librarian may even have to explain *why* the resource being suggested is a print one. Thus, the public expectations and the realities must indeed be balanced with the librarian serving as the trusted and respected guide through the abundance of reference resources that are available to the public, whether electronic or print. As much as there has been written about how the reference interview was going to be conducted in the Internet age, and how the electronic resources would replace print ones, that simply has not happened and many of the tools librarians use remain the same. For the librarian, there is much more to be aware of regarding the *number* of tools available in each format. We have *added* more to the librarian's toolkit. We have not reduced it.

With a national increase in library visits, it becomes incumbent upon library staff to participate in continuous education and learning in order to keep pace with the public's use of their libraries. Returning tens of thousands of search results from an Internet search is as useless as not finding anything at all and librarians can, and do, provide this expert guidance to provide and properly manage the information search. However, the question remains, "How does today's librarian find time to access continuing education when there is so much more to do?"

According to the American Library Association,

> While communities across the country plan their annual celebration of National Library Week [April 18-24], public library visits have reached an all-time high. In the past decade, visits have more than doubled to almost 1.2 billion, and a record-setting 1.79 billion items were borrowed from libraries in one year alone.[2]

This picture has placed an enormous amount of pressure on library staff to satisfy their institution's training and education requirements wherever and whenever they can. While e-learning may not be their first choice to satisfy that need, it may well be their *only* choice.

If, that is so, and e-learning is a librarian's only training choice, there are challenges to be met, not the least of which is technofear or the simple inability to physically connect with a human learning source. To that end, the UCLA extension program offers a somewhat Kafkaesque scenario regarding the very real fear of the adult learner entering the often baffling world of e-learning environment on his or her first day:

> There's a large corkboard on one wall and across the room is a row of twenty or so lockers, each with a person's name on it. Each locker has sort of a mail-slot large enough to deposit notes or similar items. On the corkboard is a friendly note to the class from your instructor along with a copy of her lecture. Your instructor invites you all to come back within the next few days and pin onto the board any questions or comments you have about the lecture, the class, or anything related to the class.[3]

This scenario, while ostensibly extreme, can be very real to those entering the realm of e-learning. After all, the contact appears in the omnipresence of e-mail or chat and the materials for the training are all available online. There is no personal collegiality with classmates, except through virtual means and here only written contact with the instructor, or at worst, there is no instructor at all and the material is simply established as a series of online lessons to which one must interact through a series of click-through modules. It appears cold and impersonal. However, in reality, there is actually *greater* and more sustained connection by the e-learning student than the traditional classroom student.

In an e-learning environment, students may find that there is an expectation that, because there is no direct synchronous encounter between student and instructor, that the assignments will be uncomplicated and less demanding. The challenge in this case is to create an understanding in the student that, because there is no physical manifestation of an instructor to lead or guide the class, there is no discipline involved in taking the class, nor little demanded of them to complete it.

In order to avoid such a perception, it is imperative that students in an online environment understand at the outset that this observation is entirely incorrect. E-learning must be viewed as a visible and constant presence so that the students grasp the concept that the expectations of them completing their work, as self-motivated individuals, are just as important as if there was an instructor standing before them. The student must also appreciate that in the system of asynchronous e-learning, the student must assume responsibility for his or her own interaction with expected course activities. The course syllabus and schedule are very structured in terms of timelines, deadlines, participation, and attendance. If the learner's tendency is to procrastinate, or if the learner is not self-motivated, then this is not the appropriate learning platform for him or her. Finally, if the learner simply does not have the time to devote to the online course, which will inevitably require multiple postings each week to satisfy the participation requirement, then this is definitely not the appropriate learning platform for him or her.

Attendance and active participation is even more of a challenge in the online environment than it is in the traditional classroom simply because in the former, there will be students who are uncomfortable not only with the course content and its required assignments, but with the online technology itself. This may pose an additional challenge for the instructor, for it may compound a student's unwillingness to participate appropriately. The students may think of themselves as less qualified to learn in such an environment because of their lack of technical expertise, and they may fear that this inadequacy may hamper their progress. This could pose an additional challenge simply because of the enormity of the time expenditure that may be necessary for individual students to become experienced with the technology aspects of the course, to then finally become comfortable enough with the environment so that they may function adequately. So, it becomes the added responsibility of the e-learning courseware to be as intuitive and user-friendly as possible so as not to turn off perspective students.

While it is the task of the provider's information technology support department to serve as a resource for questions regarding technological support, the student library learner's first contact when a course begins is the training coordinator or human capacity development specialist in his or her own library. The role of that individual is to provide guidance for the course and/or workshop opportunities that are available to the library learner. If the "live" classroom training is not an acceptable option, e-learning may indeed be the choice for that person.

Once engaged in the e-learning course and/or workshop module, it is the duty of the instructor to provide guidance to students who are having difficulties with the technological aspects of the course, but there may be little more than a help desk to assist students, offering support, but little in the way of individual instruction. Questions that may appear to have obvious answers to the fully trained instructor may not be as obvious to students. So, such actions as posting messages with attachments, understanding when to use a threaded message as opposed to a stand-alone message must be explained.

For library learners with limited computer skills, they may require additional guidance regarding the e-learning modules in which they are expected to work. For example, if a student understands that Microsoft Word and Microsoft Excel is preinstalled on his or her computer, he or she may not be aware that Microsoft PowerPoint is installed as well, and never would have learned to use it unless required to do so. So, if a course or workshop assignment requires PowerPoint, they may ask where they can purchase such a software product, not knowing that they already have it with them. So, in addition to instructing students in the content of the training course, there may well be a considerable effort involved in being comfortable with the technology as well.

Often, in the online setting, courses may be compressed into as few as four or five modules. Unlike the traditional classroom where there may be a single class meeting for several hours, the online classroom requires the student's presence more often so that completion is achieved in a reasonable amount of time. There is also often the expectation that, in certain courses and or workshops, because there is no instructor monitoring the student's progress (since the course or workshop may be completely self-guided), that one does not have to expend a substantial effort into completing the assignments in as timely a manner as the traditional classroom student, then he or she may wish to reconsider their choice, and return to the traditional instructor-led classroom.

Active participation in an online course may also be defined much differently from that of the traditional classroom student. For example, participation in an online course is not simply a student's cursory on-line posting of a greeting to one's classmates, or a discussion about the weather in his or her location. In addition to completing the as-signments, the student must read, analyze, and respond to the ques-tions and comments posed by the course syllabus, and, if possible, interact with the allied chat rooms associated with each particular module of learning in a mediated chat room setting. In other words, students are expected to do more than just submit their assignments; they must enthusiastically participate in the coursework and in the chat rooms in order to fully receive the value of the course.

An additional challenge to communication and, thus, to learning as well in the e-learning environment can be the concept of proper online etiquette, or "netiquette." According to author Virginia Shea, there are ten basic rules of netiquette:

> Rule 1: Remember the human.
> Rule 2: Adhere to the same standards of behavior online that you follow in real life.
> Rule 3: Know where you are in cyberspace.
> Rule 4: Respect other people's time and bandwidth.
> Rule 5: Make yourself look good online.
> Rule 6: Share expert knowledge.
> Rule 7: Help keep flame wars under control.
> Rule 8: Respect other people's privacy.
> Rule 9: Don't abuse your power.
> Rule 10: Be forgiving of other people's mistakes.[4]

Adult learners often have a great deal of "real world" knowledge. Such a wealth of experience is a great benefit to the staffer participat-ing in e-learning to offer in their selected courses. Students come from an array of backgrounds, and often enter class equipped with a com-plete toolkit of experience learned in the workplace. Such experience can serve to greatly benefit them as they may often be able to readily relate "real world" experiences into all activities and discussions.

Although e-learning as a concept may be considered by the library as a replacement for traditional classroom education and training, the statistics have not supported it. It is the rare institution where greater than 30 percent of the staff participate in online learning. That figure may not rise in the foreseeable future as the popularity of the "blended" learning model, involving a planned combination of approaches has taken hold as the preferable method of providing staff with lifelong learning opportunities.

When adult students enter the online learning environment, many of them expect a similar setting. Unfortunately, the truth can appear very different from the expectation. Depending on the vendor selected by the library and the online learning system (OLS) selected, learning platforms may be very different in look and feel and functionality. Therefore, often, the training coordinator can serve as the primary guide to direct the library learner in understanding how to successfully negotiate the OLS that has been selected. Even if there is a self-guided training module that can serve to teach the library learner how to negotiate the OLS, depending on one's own learning style, it may be more beneficial to be "walked" through the system by a "live" trainer.

In addition, if an individual arrives with the expectation that there is less work in the online environment, and that one does not have to expend a significant effort into completing the assignments, then he or she may wish to reconsider his or her method of study. The fact is, there is a great deal more work and interaction among the students in the online environment than there is in the classroom setting. After all, when students attend class in a classroom setting, they will generally attend a single evening each week. However, in the online learning environment, where student interaction may be required as many as four or five days each week, the continuous learning environment of such a class may simply prove too difficult for some students to handle, especially if that student has not been in a classroom for some time in recent years.

Though the content of an online course may be enough to dissuade the student to continue, especially if that student has not written much in recent years and finds himself or herself in a situation where writing is the primary method of communication, it may simply be the technology that blocks the learning process.

It has been said that when the economy goes south, registrations in higher education go north. If that is the case, then the number of students entering the higher education online environment will lead to a flood, not only of inexperienced students, but also of inexperienced computer users. For the online facilitator, such a double-edged level of inexperience can be a deadly combination, both for facilitator and student. The facilitator ends up expending almost as much effort in working with the student in learning how to technically negotiate the online environment as one does working with the student to properly prepare his or her assignments.

In a white paper written by the OCLC E-Learning Task Force, the need for e-learning opportunities in libraries was expressed:

> The Task Force also voiced a significant need for better and more focused training—for librarians, for faculty and for students. The challenge of establishing relevant, yet scalable training is not new to librarians and there is now the possibility of embedding training support within the learning management system as a part of the learning activity. The idea of "just enough-just-in-time-just-for-me" was seen as a desirable objective.[5]

This leads to a challenge for the library training and development program design team. Because the fragile financial nature of libraries today dictates that staffing levels in many libraries are likely to continue to remain flat or even decrease over time, it is still reasonable to expect that 70 percent of training continues to occur outside of the library using the standard instructor-led classroom model. However, the approximately 30 percent of those who embrace e-learning will do so out of necessity as much as desire. This level of engagement in e-learning (30 percent) has not varied much in the last decade in the workplace, and it may take a generational shift to increase this percentage.

Finally, in order for staff to be successful, e-learning must be easily accessible, comprehensive, applicable, and meaningful. If these factors are in place, the library can then move forward with this component of the blended library learning program for its staff.

Chapter 3

Developing a Personal Learning Plan

The Challenge—Creating and Maintaining
a Realistic and Practical Learning Plan

What Is a Personal Learning Plan (PLP)?

The PLP is a means by which each employee can establish his or her own *realistic* roadmap to success as a learner. Certainly, the key word in this challenge is "realistic." Creating a *pie-in-the-sky* scenario can be a recipe for disappointment. Creating the PLP should be an annual event for each and every library learner.

At the start of each year, the learner establishes, along with his or her supervisor, a goal-oriented structure to continuous learning that is predictable, manageable, and outcome-based. That is, each individual must develop this plan with the intention of completing all that he or she sets out to do. Intentions can be derailed, given the workloads of most of us; however, if the PLP is linked as a human resources function to the annual performance review, there will be additional incentive, both philosophically and monetarily to complete one.

The PLP is a practical plan to help establish the parameters of learning for the entire year. The concept of the PLP should be implemented at the organizational level for all employees working in the library. Therefore, a template must be developed by the organization with an eye toward personalization by each employee. Although the focus in the PLP is on the word "personal," the other two terms in this concept—"learning" and "plan"—carry equal weight and validity.

If the goal of an organization is to create a continuous learning environment in the workplace *(workplace as learning place),* wherein the mission of the library itself serves as the driver for staff learning must be developed, then this awareness can become a guiding principle for the organization and a touchstone for both the library and its employees.

Basic Steps for Preparing Your Learning Plan

In preparing the learning plan, there are a number of activities, suggested by author Hal Macomber,[1] one should complete or accomplish in order to be successful. Starting with the individual's goals within the structure of the organizational goals, each employee should be encouraged to reach these goals with the expectation that the completion of continuous education established at the beginning of the year will be an important element under consideration during one's annual performance evaluation. Once the template has been established organizationally, then it becomes the responsibility of every employee to adhere to it in order to work one's way through to the plan's completion. However, it then becomes the responsibility of the organization to develop and utilize the appropriate assessment tool in order to properly and fairly assess the success of the individual. A number of tools have been developed for this use.

A particular effective assessment tool can be one that considers one's goals and individual priorities for the year in consideration of (1) institutional, (2) professional, and, of course, (3) personal development. In order to indicate a comprehensive and well-developed structure, descriptions of how the goals will be achieved and measured should also be included in the PLP.

The SMART Model

The SMART PLP model can offer an effective and flexible means of implementing the PLP. The acronym, SMART, is defined as specific, measurable, achievable, relevant, and timed.[2] Although to some, this method may appear overly structured, this template offers flexibility and creativity for the learner because it allows the learner to carefully consider each step in the model and plot the strategy he or she will find it best to employ based on one's particular skill level.

Specific

Provide enough detail so that there is no indecision as to what exactly you should be doing when the time comes to do it.

Measurable

Your goal should be such that when you are through you have some tangible evidence of completion.

Acceptable

Your goal should be set by you rather than by someone else. You know best your strengths and weaknesses, and you can use this information to maximize your chances of success.

Relevant

Do not plan to do things that you are unlikely to follow through. Give yourself some flexibility.

Timed

Say when you plan to work at your goal, for example, between 4 and 5 p.m. Anything that will take you more that two hours to complete, break into smaller, more manageable chunks.

Your PLP

The following information is designed to help you define, plan, implement, and document your learning. By preparing a learning plan, you develop a systematic approach to learning a skill or competency. The following questions will help you identify the key components of your learning plan, and the chart is a tool to "map" and document your plan.

1. *Topic or area of learning.* What skill, competency, or area of knowledge do you want to develop?
   Example A: I want to improve my ability to evaluate staff work performance.
   Example B: I want to become more proficient with using desktop applications.
2. *Current level of skill or competency.* What are your current skills in this area?
   Example A: I know how to identify strengths and weaknesses in staff performance and I generally know how staff members might improve their competencies.
   Example B: I know how to use word processing programs.

3. *Need.* What gaps or areas for improvement do you see?
    Example A: Our current approach to performance appraisal does not foster effective and meaningful communication between the supervisor and the staff about work performance.
    Example B: I do not know how to create spreadsheets.

4. *Learning goal.* Based on the need(s) you have identified above, what do you hope to accomplish as a result of your learning activity? (Be as specific as possible about what you will be able to do after completing your learning activity. When stating your goal, avoid terms that can be vague such as "understand," "know," and "learn." Use action verbs to describe your goal and focus on the results of your learning.)
    Example A: I will identify at least four new approaches for conducting performance appraisals. I will also assess which approach would work best in our library.
    Example B: I will create a spreadsheet for monitoring our department's budget.

5. *Strategies and resources.* What strategies and resources can be used to meet your learning goal? Which strategies and resources are the best matches for what you want to learn? (Be creative in thinking about possible learning strategies and resources. It is often helpful to brainstorm possible strategies and resources with colleagues.)
    Example A: Conduct a literature review to identify new models and approaches for performance appraisal. Interview five managers in other libraries who have similar responsibilities to learn about different performance appraisal strategies and methods.
    Example B: Complete an online tutorial on creating spreadsheets. Practice creating sample spreadsheets for one hour each week for four weeks.

6. *Time frame.* When will you begin and finish your learning activity?
    Example A: Complete the literature review during July 2007. Conduct interviews during August 2007. Meet with other supervisors and staff in our library to evaluate the different approaches and models during September 2007. Recommend a different approach for performance appraisals in October 2007.

Example B: Complete the tutorial during July 2007 and practice new skills during August 2007. Transfer monthly budget reports from paper format to electronic format in September 2007.

7. *Evidence of learning.* How will you know when you have reached your learning goal? (Describe what you—and perhaps others—will observe.)

Example A: I will prepare a report and recommendation about a revised or new approach for conducting performance appraisals.

Example B: The department's monthly budget reports will be maintained and produced electronically.

A Personal Commitment to Learning

Clearly, a fundamental condition of a successful PLP requires that the individual views his or her commitment to the program. This requires a personal vision that stretches out long after a single year has passed. It is recommended that one prepare one's PLP in the manner of a "living" document wherein the ability to revise and update it becomes a guiding force in its validity. There are hundreds of examples of the PLP template available on the Web. Although the data elements included may slightly differ from those designed by the library for its employees, this form can be used by the employee as a personal and flexible document that may be consulted throughout the year and updated, as necessary, to meet the goals of each individual's PLP.

In many examples of the PLP, the form is divided into three distinct sections. The results of each area of lifelong learning will affect the individual, the organization, and one's colleagues, supervisors, and staff. The first section of the PLP will often indicate the manner in which the employee's learning will impact the institutional and departmental goals. The second section will address one's professional development goals (it is in this section where the courses, workshops, e-learning opportunities, Webinars, podcasts, certifications, and the like participated in by the employee will all be documented. Finally, in section three, one's "personal development" is acknowledged and documented where one's personal goals and expectations will be documented.

This manner of self-assessment provides a clearly understood road-map to the attainment of success in continuous education. A significant ingredient in each section of this document is the "measurement" component wherein it is expected that each employee is able to indicate his or her own measure of success. Communication with one's supervisor is critical in measuring the success of lifelong learning because there may be areas where measurement of success may be assessed at a different level by the employee than by one's supervisor. It also serves as a discussion document for managers and staff to meet periodically in order to check up on the progress of the staffer. Inclusive discussion may alleviate any disconnects.

The PLP serves as an extremely empowering individual document for each employee that, once implemented, will set the foundation for the lifelong learning for each employee in manageable, realistic, organized, and measurable portions.

Chapter 4

The Substitute Librarian—
Providing a Mechanism
for the Library Learner to Learn

The Challenge—Creating a Flexible
Alternative Staffing Model

Although the substitute teacher and the adjunct professor have become fixtures in our education system, the concept of the substitute librarian has not been readily embraced as a solution to libraries experiencing short staffing issues. While not a particularly new concept, substitute librarians have been used as temporary employees to fill in when permanent staff are on leave from their libraries for health, maternal, vacation, personal, or other reasons.

Although not as acute as the level of job loss in many industries in the private sector, libraries too have been presented with cuts or, often, level funding, either freezing current positions or no longer filling the positions of those who have resigned or retired. Still, according to The Hay Group, "Given the number of jobs that have been eliminated in the past five years without a commensurate reduction in work, the expectations of those remaining are such that it is difficult for these roles to be successful."[1] The environment in libraries where this has occurred has not only limited the training opportunities for remaining staff, but also made the option of training nearly impossible.

Library administrators must seek creative solutions if they are to provide continuous training to staff under such circumstances. One suggestion is to create the "substitute" role so that permanent employees may be temporarily replaced so they may attend outside training when necessary.

The following is an example of a substitute librarian's job description illustrating the job characteristics and the job requirements of an individual being sought to fill such a position for the Montana State Library.

Job Characteristics

Work with the public and other staff members.
Perform the list of duties for all staff members.
Dress in a professional manner.
Keep busy doing jobs from the list of everyday duties.
Follow the regular policies and procedures of the library.

Job Requirements

Knowledge: A working knowledge of library principles, organization, operation, and procedures.

Skills and abilities: Circulation of books, library equipment, communication skills, work well with others, work on your own, and carry on tasks without being told.[2]

If the library has adopted the concept of lifelong learning for its staff but often finds it difficult to send staff members to off-site instructor-led training sessions, one possible approach is to hire part-time staff on a "substitute" basis to rely on when permanent staff is assigned to attend training classes. This chapter examines the concept of "The Substitute Librarian" and some of the wider implications of implementing such a process.

However, let us leave the world of libraries for a moment, but not the world of lifelong learning, by applying a simple baseball scenario to serve as a metaphor for this concept.

You are the manager of a baseball team playing in the league championship playoff series. The winner of this game will go to the World Series if you win. Your team is down by one run. There is a runner at third base and it is two-out. The inning is, of course, the bottom of the ninth. The pitcher has been brilliant through nine innings, but finally appears to be tiring. Your next scheduled batter is a player who is not known as a clutch hitter, therefore, not particularly a threat. However, in professional baseball, the game can turn on anyone's momentary stroke of genius (note Bucky Dent in 1978 and Aaron Boone in 2003). Still, as a responsible manager, you must assign a pinch hitter to bat for the scheduled batter. You have two choices for pinch hitter. One is a solid, reliable player who was once a great one but who has fallen into a slump and does not play everyday anymore. The other is a power hitter who strikes out as much as he hits home runs. One could potentially tie the game with a hit, and the other can win the game with a home run. Either of them can fall victim to whatever strength the pitcher can summon to get through this game and strike out and your team goes home until next season. Who do you put in as the pinch hitter?

Well, while you are left to ponder what you would do in such circumstances, let us return to the concept of the substitute library staff member—the pinch hitter, if you will—and the many possibilities there may be to implement such a concept in your library.

As a library manager, facing the issue of lack of adequate staff to fill your full-time ranks of employees, where will you find *additional* professional staff to fill in so permanent staff can attend training? Where will these part-timers come from? Here are some suggestions:

Recent graduates seeking their MLS or recent MLS graduates seeking a second degree who do not wish to work or cannot work full-time

Single parents (who cannot work full-time)

School Media Specialists who may not work evenings or weekends

Full-time MLS staff working at other libraries seeking supplementary income.

What about paraprofessionals and/or support staff? These employees must also attend training to sharpen or upgrade their skills. Who can pinch hit for them? How about:

Single parents

Parents seeking a second income with flexible hours

People with public service skills

People willing to work nights and weekends
People willing to work only mornings
People willing to work only afternoons
Teachers (especially in summer)
MLS or other graduate students
Undergraduate students
People willing to work on short notice
Actors and other disciplines with flexible and/or short notice
   availability
People seeking a part-time job with benefits.

Flexibility is clearly the key word in seeking out these part-time staffers. Not only for the individuals, but for the library as well. These substitutes must not be seen only as personnel who remain on-call in case of emergencies. Such schemes have been attempted before and abandoned because the substitutes were only relied upon in emergency situations. The concept in this case is very different. Training must be an established part of everyone's job description and seen as a continuous process, thus the need for continuous substitutes replacing staff at training becomes a standard operating procedure in the day-to-day operations of the library. *Continuous training* is a key word in this instance, not only for permanent staff, but also for substitutes.

Cross-Training of Substitutes

In order for substitute staff to "hit the ground running," so to speak, training must be available immediately for potential substitutes. However, not only training for the jobs that they will substitute, but also for those they *might* substitute in the future. Therefore, cross-training is imperative for substitute staff. Cross-trained staff can be an extremely valuable staffing component of the library.

Cross-training achieves the following objectives:

Prevents stagnation
Offers a learning and professional development opportunity
Rejuvenates all departments
Improves understanding of the different departments
Leads to better coordination and teamwork
Erases differences, enmity, and unhealthy competition

Increases knowledge, know-how, skills, and work performance
Improves overall motivation
Leads to the sharing of organizational goals and objectives.[3]

"Today, most organizations [including libraries] are complex mosa-
ics representing dynamic combinations of operating and support func-
tions, business units and alliances."[4]

Cross-training may take anywhere from a few hours to a few days to
even a few weeks, depending on the level of cross-training expected by
the library. For example, if the substitute is a reference librarian hired
to fill in for other reference librarians, the training will be minimal.
However, if the substitute holds an MLS and has worked in several
areas of the library, these staffers may be able to serve as *generalists*
and fill in at any of the necessary MLS positions that are open. These
cross-trained staffers can easily move between departments to fill in
whatever role may be necessary to fill in times of permanent staff outage because of outside training.

There is an additional benefit of having substitute staff float between departments. Such generalists may also serve to highlight the
reliance that one department of the library shares with another. These
employees may move between the departments, and in a subtle manner serve to increase the library's overall morale. Permanent staff who
may not have thought much about the reliance that one department has
upon another, and the nature of what those dependencies mean for the
library as a cohesive entity may begin to understand the interrelated
nature of each department and its inclusive relationship to the library.
There is a great shared sense of mission and the individual's place
within the organization does not need to be singularly and strictly
defined.

Budget Implications of Hiring Substitutes

There is, of course, a budgetary implication in creating the substitute role. However, if finances necessary to support this concept are
measured against the value received by having a well-trained staff,
the cost/benefit of doing so may be advantageous.

In times of short staffing in libraries, a constant since this writer has
been a librarian (more than two decades), it becomes imperative to

review strategies for maximizing the full-time staff. In order to accomplish this, an annual review of all staff positions must be conducted. By conducting such an "environmental" scan of the staff positions, the library will readily uncover training practices not addressed, and perhaps a large number of staff who received no training whatsoever. Inconsistencies in the staff skills may also be uncovered. In which case, it is wise for the library administration to take a step back and explore alternatives to lack of proper training. Reviewing and improving library structure and the design of individual jobs can increase staff motivation.

It is often assumed that because the library appears fully staffed on paper all of its people are in place all of the time. This, of course, is never the case. It is often speculated that, in the library, there is anywhere between a 17 to 20 percent outage on any one day because of illness, vacation, personal days, emergencies, and, of course, training days. These numbers, of course, are not much different in the private sector. Therefore, the obvious need for staff redundancy ought to be uppermost in the minds of administrators who expect to provide the best customer service using staff who have not been to training refresher courses, and who are overworked because of long hours and short staff issues.

Although previous suggestions regarding who might be included in the pool of potential substitutes included a number of people who will, undoubtedly, not be conversant in the language of libraries as well as the processes and policies designed to dictate the procedures of the workflow, it would certainly benefit the library to hire those who are already knowledgeable. These individuals would require less training and many of them could hit the ground running, so to speak, on their first day of work, rather than have to attend rigorous and/or lengthy training sessions prior to facing the public. There is always a certain level of training required for new employees, but if these "new" employees are conversant in the *lingua franca* of libraries, there will certainly be less training necessary at the outset for them. Also, there is great currency in having a set of guidelines, rules, and procedures for each department. In having these fully documented, there will already be a volume (perhaps several) of material to support the substitute, and to which he or she may refer in questions of procedure, especially where there is a technological process that must be employed. Therefore, technology training is especially important when there is a specialized system in place. Though the substitute may have understood a system *like* the one he or she will be working with, it is imperative to understand the *exact* system with which he or she will be working. In technology training, quite often, there are no shortcuts. Specific procedures must be learned and understood. If such training procedures can be replicated in a Web-based environment, then the procedural components may be mixed with the practical elements when the substitute is actually assigned to a service location in the library. There are often many useful online help tools available to support user training. These may be employed to offer an extra level of comfort for new employees.

The Positive Impact of a Graying Profession

There has been a great deal written about the "graying" of the library workforce. Most of what has been written has been done with a vision of a stark "doom and gloom" scenario. Will potential substitutes be enticed to return to the workplace from the ranks of retirees holding an MLS expected to retire as the baby boomers reach retirement age? Is this a viable option? How many employees will want to return to the workplace after having spent a lifetime of service? Perhaps more than retiring professionals from other professions might consider.

As an example, in 2002, the Institute of Museum and Library Services (IMLS) awarded a two-year grant to the Chicago Library System, a library consortium, an $80,000 grant to train twenty-four librarians nearing retirement to become "consultant-coaches" to forty-eight library staff most likely to move into management and specialized positions. The project was also designed to create a Web-based learning resource to support coaching and staff retention efforts in the library profession.

Also, many librarians are more than willing to serve on committees in the professional library associations for some time after they have retired. Still others begin a successful, if only part-time, consulting practice upon retirement. So, many of us appear to keep a hand in the profession, even though we have "officially" retired. This is good news for library systems all across the country that are expected to experience a 30 to 40 percent loss of their professional and leadership staff in the next five years. In terms of succession training of younger staff for positions of authority in libraries upon the retirement of so many, we can look forward to a reasonably smooth transition if these "retired" librarians return to the workplace as part-time mentors, coaches, consultants, and substitute librarians. The other side of this argument, of course, is that the profession must actively continue to recruit new holders of the MLS if this scenario is to be successful.

Chapter 5

Marketing Your Library Learning Program to Staff

The Challenge—Creating an Interesting, Relevant, and Continuous Internal Marketing Program That Delivers

No successful service can continue to appeal to its audience without the continuous reinvention and refining of that service and the equally continuous input of its users. In supporting the concept of "workplace as learning place," it is necessary to market continuing education and training to library staff not only at the roll out phase but in an ongoing manner throughout the year, not only to those who have already bought in to the program but also to those who have either excused themselves from the program or have not seen fit to previously investigate its intellectual and practical significance. It is often wrongly assumed that there is no need to market a program to library staff already actively involved in it. Internal marketing just by virtue of its existence should be enough of a tool to drive the marketing initiative. Unfortunately, that is usually not the case. Those who make such assumptions are often surprised when staff usage of the program drops or when instructor-led classes are only sporadically attended. As anyone working in a library today can attest to, library staff have so much on their plates these days that it is often quite a burden to take part in the library learning program, no matter how comprehensive it may be.

Although word of mouth is often the best and least expensive device in the marketer's toolkit, the benefits of the library learning program may not have been sufficiently promoted amongst the library staff. Conversely, knowing the reasons for lack of participation in the program are often as important to training administrators as is information about those who *are* involved in it. Even the most vigorous campaign, if improperly targeted, will meet with a stony silence and expire if the program has not been continually marketing using a variety of methods. If library learning has not been viewed as merely a "frill" and it has finally been embraced both by library management and library staff, it is imperative that the training administrators perform a number of ongoing tasks to keep interest and excitement high through a regular schedule of marketing campaigns to reinvigorate the program.

Since most training administrators have not generally received formal education in marketing, it would benefit individuals to perform a self-check of marketing competencies in order to acquaint themselves with the skills necessary to roll out and sustain a successful library learning marketing campaign. Also, such a self-check is valuable in terms of uncovering any additional formal training required by the training administrator.

According to authors Sophie Oberstein and Jan Alleman, there are fourteen marketing competencies with which one ought to be familiar prior to embarking an active marketing process for learning. These are

> Relationship building
> Comprehension of organizational and individual behavior
> Knowledge of your audience
> Knowledge of your topic or field
> Creativity
> Intellectual versatility
> Cost-benefit analysis
> Trends and data analysis
> Questioning technique
> Project planning
> Maintenance evaluation
> Written and verbal presentation
> Graphic design
> Computer proficiency.[1]

In order to reinforce these competencies through a recommended and accepted strategy, the training administrator may wish to employ a commonly referred to Instructional Systems Design (ISD) model known as ADDIE.

The acronym, ADDIE, represents these five components:

- Analyze
- Design
- Development
- Implementation
- Evaluation.

> *Analyze* phase—instructional problem clarified, goals and objectives are established, and the learning environment and learner characteristics identified.
>
> *Design* phase—instructional strategies are designed and media choices are made.
>
> *Develop* phase—materials are produced according to decisions made during the design phase.
>
> *Implement* phase—testing of prototypes [with targeted audience], putting the [service] in full production, and training learners and instructors on how to use (it).
>
> *Evaluation* phase consists of two parts. *Formative* evaluation is present in each stage. *Summative* evaluation—tests for criterion-related referenced items—providing opportunities for feedback from users.[2]

As one of more than 100 recommended ISDs, the ADDIE model can be used for the creation of the *entire* training program, rather than using it to concentrate solely on the marketing of that program. In a sense, though, the reinvention of the entire program, over the course of time, is very much the point of utilizing an inclusive process such as this. When simplified for use as the underpinning for marketing the library learning program, the framework of ADDIE provides the program administrator with a solid foundation wherein the entire training program's creation, implementation, and marketing are all based on the same unified model. This approach provides an important level of consistency across the entire spectrum of the education and training program. These components, if employed properly and reliably, can impart a level of interaction with library staff so that one does not implement a learning program in a void.

It should be noted that the utilization of the ADDIE model has, at times, provoked an adverse effect among training program designers. Some have suggested that the process is an extremely cumbersome and rigid approach to systems design. However, when employed as the engine driving the marketing of a library learning program, this framework allows for the logical process from which to proceed toward a stated goal of providing the staff with a program in which they have been a part of that design approach.

It is already difficult enough to bring people to the table in agreement over what serves as a measurable, sustainable model of a learning program. But, by using the components of ADDIE, it becomes clearer to administrators that those who are using the training program believe in its worth, thereby providing a justification regarding an education and training program's sustainability.

(A)nalyze in Preparation for Marketing the Staff Training Program

This is the first step in this process and it is imperative, not only to uncover the actual need, rather than the perceived need, but also to begin to generate interest and excitement in the training program in those who will participate in it. By conducting the needs assessment for training issues, it is wise to consider not only those areas of concern regarding training program content, but other logistical matters as well. As described in the next chapter's case study, the Southeast Florida Library Information Network (SEFLIN) employs a "blended learning" solution to its more than 3,000 staff working in its member libraries. In order to assess the level of need for its upcoming year's program, it is essential to uncover what the needs are, directly from the staff participating in the program. They will be the stakeholders in the program and their voice ought to speak loudly in this process. Therefore, a short, simple, but effective needs assessment survey based on the SEFLIN "blended learning" model may be distributed to staff in order to collect important needs data (see Exhibit 5.1).

From this survey, the data collected will be used to create programs based directly on staff needs. Also, logistical items such as the time of day, the location, and the delivery methods for the workshops, tutorials, and courses most requested will be closely analyzed in order

EXHIBIT 5.1 Needs assessment survey

1. What delivery method(s) would you *most prefer* to use? (check all that apply)

   ☐ Web based (online)
   ☐ Instructor led
   ☐ Teleconference
   ☐ VHS video
   ☐ Streaming media (online)

2. What times of the day are better for you to participate in classes, workshops, or tutorials? (check only one)

   ☐ A.M. (mornings)
   ☐ P.M. (afternoons)
   ☐ Full day (morning and afternoon)

3. I am interested in attending classes, workshops, or tutorials for career advancement or professional enhancement.

   ☐ No
   ☐ Yes (If "yes," please suggest topics of interest.)

4. I am willing to attend classes, workshops, or tutorials at the following locations (check all that apply)

   ☐ A library in my county
   ☐ A teleconference site in my county
   ☐ A CompUSA training lab in my county
   ☐ A library, teleconference site, or lab outside my county

5. At the library I work in, I have access to a library staff computer that I can use to take online classes, workshops, or tutorials.

   ☐ No
   ☐ Yes

6. At work, I have time to take online classes, workshops, or tutorials.

   ☐ No
   ☐ Yes

7. I would like further training in computer skills.

   ☐ No
   ☐ Yes (If "yes," list those skills)

(continued)

(continued)

8. Are there challenges that will make it difficult for you to participate in classes, workshops, or tutorials?

☐ No
☐ Yes (If "yes," please list those challenges)

9. What staff development or training classes, workshops, or tutorials would be most helpful for you *in the coming year*? (please list below)

10. My position is

☐ Administrator
☐ Librarian
☐ Library Assistant
☐ Clerical
☐ Information Technology (or Systems)
☐ Public Relations
☐ Accountant
☐ Graduate Intern
☐ Other (LTA, Admin Assistant, Library Specialist, etc.)

to assure maximum participation by library staff. Clearly, if the logistical information returned indicates the most preferred times of day and locations of instructor-led training classes and the program administrators ignore this information, they will be providing training in a vacuum and the instructors will be working in mostly empty rooms.

Library administrators must be responsive to the travel and scheduling issues of the library staff. If a considerable number of staff expresses their concern that they cannot attend training for a particular reason (short staffing, scheduling problems, travel issues, etc.), the program administrators must be cognizant of such information. Perhaps a response to such issues would be to offer more Web-based training where participants can access training online, or through increased use of teleconferencing, where many people can visit a single location and view a program at the same time. Even a videotape course may be suggested so that an individual or a group may receive training through this very traditional method. The point is that the "blended learning" solution offers numerous methods for staff to access training, and in so doing, interest in the program and program usage can remain reinvigorated.

While the "E" in ADDIE stands for "evaluation," this has more to do with the evaluation of the content than it does with the needs assessment or "analysis." Therefore, the results of this survey ought to be promoted to staff and used very much as a marketing tool so that when the program is developed for the coming year, the stakeholders really feel as though they have played a valuable part in the creation of that program, because they have!

(D)esign the Marketing Program

In a similar manner to the building of a successful overall "blended learning" program where a number of various methods are employed to deliver course content to library staff, the marketing for the learning program must likewise employ a plethora of strategies and tools to be effective.

According to author Teresa Davenport, there are four distinct elements to set in place prior to deciding which tools are necessary to employ as marketing items targeted to staff engaged in the training program. These are

Product—determining just what programs are required.

Price—marketing's role to promote the cost-effectiveness of the program, both in terms of its benefits to the organization and its production cost.

Place—programs need to be easily accessible to learners.

Promotion of communication—the major tools you will use.[3]

One must have developed a budget for marketing so that the items necessary to create as marketing tools may be purchased. As has been mentioned earlier, within the library, the best marketing tool is word of mouth. The program's best salespeople are those who are using it extensively and are pleased with its outcomes for them personally. If they have received any incentives upon completion of any of their training, then their positive response to the training program will be even greater. Therefore, within the marketing budget it is wise to plan for some incentives or rewards to present to those who have success-fully completed training modules. Even if the incentives are limited to framed certificates of completion and acknowledgment of an indi-vidual's success is noted in one's personnel folder that is the kind of incentive that can be translated into rewards down the line. Here are some practical suggestions for marketing during the design phase.

Use the library's e-mail or intranet system to promote the library learning program.

You can use the e-mail or the intranet (if there is one in place) to publicize specific courses, new courses, offer useful tips and helpful suggestions for incorporating learning into employees' personal de-velopment. Regular promotion to staff regarding new and exciting learning program offerings may encourage those who have not par-ticipated in the program to consider it.

Printed materials (handouts, brochures, information cards, plac-ards, stickers, etc.) are still very effective. Flyers and newsletters may be a consideration.

The best approach, especially in marketing a blended learning program, is to design and send out marketing materials in as many methods as possible. Since there will be a considerable number of employees who respond better to more traditional marketing materials, such as handouts or printed newsletters, this may be a more effective means of increasing usage in the learning program rather than strictly to e-communication.

Work with your learning vendors.

For obvious reasons, it is in their best interest to work with you to assist in providing support with internal marketing. Furthermore, they may have already designed marketing materials that you can either adapt or directly distribute to staff touting the benefits of the learning program or elements of it.

Three critical elements in the design of the overall program will in-clude budget, timeline, and staff available to produce the materials and promote the program. As is often the case, even in larger library systems, the program administrator is a single individual, and if for-tunate, may be assigned an assistant. Where there are less than the de-sired availability of resources, it is imperative that the training program administrator is creative in developing multiple pathways to learning including partnering with other libraries for better costs, grant funding of training programs, and developing many in-house opportunities using the expertise within the library system itself to provide numerous training opportunities for staff:

> Ask a staff member to share information about a professional program attended or schedule a discussion about a hot topic.
> Establish reciprocal agreements with neighboring libraries to share trainers. Send staff to each other's programs.
> Volunteer to host a workshop.
> Consider adapting staff development materials from other programs for use in your library. LAMA maintains a clearinghouse of staff development materials, programs, and policies (http://www.ala.org/lama/committees/hrs/information.html). There may be trainers available for free through your city, county, or other parent institution (community college, university, corporation.)
> Train someone on your staff to be a trainer.[4]

(D)evelopment of the Marketing Program Materials

According to Teresa Davenport, "Once you have determined what the marketing mix of your promotions will be, you can begin producing the actual materials."[5]

In developing marketing materials such as a brochure, it becomes obvious that a great many other materials may be designed using the copy created for that brochure. Also, the look and feel of the brochure can be replicated in other handouts, banners, posters, and giveaways, as well as the ability to send it out as an electronic marketing tool. Therefore, when the marketing budget has been finalized and the program administrator knows the three elements mentioned previously (budget, timeline, and staff), the organization for the design is in place and the creation of the materials can begin.

Since we are assuming that the program administrator has either limited or no marketing training, there are a number of cogent suggestions to consider when sitting down to create marketing copy for the brochure and allied marketing materials. Oberstein and Alleman suggest the following:

> Be truthful
> Know your audience

    Be culturally relevant
    Variety is the key
    Make marketing positive
    Require a response
    Stress benefits, not features
    Support with statistics
    Have themes
    Have something new to offer
    Pique their interest
    Write simply
    Use the active voice
    Pilot your copy (with others prior to finalizing).[6]

To sum this section, therefore, as you prepare the marketing materials you must present the library learning program as relevant to the staff, and by touting its many benefits, it becomes much more of an easy sell.

(I)mplementation of the Marketing Program

You must introduce the new learning program to the library (the launch) to promote it and register initial users (internal marketing) to develop ways to maintain and increase usage over time (maintenance marketing). Use the following techniques to increase excitement of the program during and after its implementation phase.

Program administrators hold a learning "rollout event."

A special event or series of events may be held to introduce staff to the library learning program. The participants may receive small premiums (mouse pads, key chains, bags, writing tablets, pens, etc.) and obtain information about the program. A mix of presentation activities may be held including hands-on demos of the program's e-courses, a slideshow demonstrating the benefits of participating in the program including descriptions of the recognition and rewards one may receive, and time for attendees to meet with the program administrators to ask questions.

Incorporate online courses into employee development, core competencies, and performance improvement plans.

Incorporating learning into one of these processes can be helpful. This can be decided at the administrative level and discussed with the employees during their annual performance review conferences. There will be greater success of the learning program if learning benchmarks are built into these monitored processes.

Provide incentive lunches during a workshop.

Managers, supervisors, and training administrators may be invited for a meeting on how to incorporate learning into their own development plans, and how they can use it in employee development and performance improvement. Show the attendees how learning can be integrated into developing, coaching, and mentoring activities.

Include a learning options discussion and a program overview into your new employee orientation program.

At the very least, give new employees an overview of your organization's learning philosophy, the options available, and how to sign up and get started.

There must be help available.

If staff have questions or difficulties (registering for a course, forgotten password, etc.), make it easy for them to get answers. The link on the library learning Web page must be prominently displayed and the help must be responsive in their replies.

Hold an annual awards ceremony.

Though a series of standard recognition methods (plaques, certificates, newsletter mentions, etc.) may be employed to recognize excellence in utilization of the learning program, the library might consider holding an annual awards ceremony where invited guests would be on hand to honor those who have demonstrated excellence in the program.

(E)valuation of the Marketing Program

The program administrator must regularly encourage feedback from those active stakeholders in the program through program evaluations or program segment evaluations (in order to analyze certain areas of a blended learning program employing several methods of content delivery) in order to understand the strengths and weaknesses of the library learning program. Those evaluations can be formal evaluations or simple phone calls to random employees once they have completed the course. Survey employees to find out what topics interest them, and consider ways to incorporate those interests into your program offerings. If you work in a larger library, seek out additional feedback from all departments.

Of course, the evaluations will return results that can be used for tweaking the campaign for the following year; therefore, the usage statistics can and should be used as marketing tools in and of themselves. These statistics can lend relevancy and stature to the program, thus helping to build its audience. You will also learn how participants learn, thus allowing the program administrator to add or delete appropriate program content, as is necessary.

A 2001 study of e-learning, titled, "If They Build It, Will They Come?" produced by the American Society for Training and Development (ASTD) and The MASIE Center revealed three critical success factors in determining whether an employee will or will not accept and participate in a work-related e-learning course. (But these findings can just as easily apply to traditional methods of workplace related learning.) These include

> Internal marketing—Employees respond better to learning when it is promoted well in advance, and they feel prepared.
> Support—Employees value and respond to learning when they feel they have the necessary technical, subject matter, and managerial support.
> Incentives—Employees respond to learning when they can clearly see the value of what they will learn.[7]

In the end, the purpose of the evaluation, whether it is accomplished through the use of surveys, questionnaires, interviews, focus groups, or one-to-one exchanges, should all seek the findings that lead to the measurable outcome of the "effectiveness" of the library learning program.

> Once you have evaluated the effectiveness of your marketing strategy . . . this will be your moment of truth because it allows you to make decisions regarding future efforts, programs and how to market new and current programs. You will also have a better knowledge base of who your audience is and why they attend training and learning programs.[8]

Chapter 6

The Community of Learning
Program for Library Staff:
The SEFLIN Case Study

The Challenge—Creating a Successful Blended
Learning Program for a Large Staff Working
in Many South Florida Libraries

A commitment to continuing education and professional development for library staff is a commitment to the future of libraries. Continuous learning is critical to renewing the expertise and
skills needed to teach and assist the public in navigating the electronic resources of the information age. The need for this education grows exponentially as the shortage of trained library staff
becomes more acute; we must retrain experienced librarians and
provide education for those non-librarians who come to work
with us. We need to recruit and build for the future of libraries.

Quote attributed to Miriam Pollack
of Miriam Pollack Associates

Lifelong learning in libraries requires that the learning experience
be built into the job description of each and every staff member. Learning benchmarks must be established within those job descriptions
through "core competencies" and a review of those benchmarks must
be accomplished annually so that the knowledge gained from one's
engagement in the program of lifelong learning in libraries is maintained. The sustainability of continuing education and training lies in

the concept that learning is not an isolated experience, but that it be viewed as an integral part of every staff member's responsibility.

To support this commitment, Southeast Florida Library Information Network (SEFLIN) sought to create a Web site to fill the need to transform the library learning culture in Southeast Florida libraries into a "Community of Learning." SEFLIN no longer viewed continuing education as simply a series of workshops or programs, but a fully integrated lifelong learning experience built into the library culture. It was necessary that the concept of "workplace as learning place" must take hold of the library and its philosophy infused into each and every staff member working and learning in that library.

There was recognition that, as the consortium's most valuable deliverable, learning had to become an essential element of each person's daily work. The environment of each library must support learning for it to be successful. It must be a valued part of what people do. It must be a *fruitful* activity. Building a learning culture means overcoming the perception that learning and work are different.

It is with this concept in mind that the SEFLIN set out to create a Web site in order to foster the concept of not simply a compilation or courses taken haphazardly, without any goal in mind, but to include all courses, workshops, tutorials, conferences, and institutes as an integrated system of learning whereby any staff member working in a SEFLIN member library would be able to participate in this *Community of Learning Program (CLP)*.

The goal of the *CLP* Web site was to emphasize the importance of a blended learning approach to continuing education for library staff and the interdependence of its parts, in other words, to create a *systems* rather than a single approach to learning. SEFLIN sought to provide tools to help staff members explore the learning needs of their organizations as well as their own learning needs and to help individual members create their own learning journeys and the best ways to meet those needs. The SEFLIN *CLP* Web site would assist members in finding a variety of learning resources. Their choices depend on content, learning style, available technology, time, and funding.

In order to lay the groundwork for this project, it was necessary to create a "functional outline" so that there could be a roadmap created to include all of the components of the Web site. In conjunction with the Web developer such a document would be created with two distinct elements: the functional requirements (these "are presented in scenarios that depict an operational system from the perspective of its end users. Included are one or more examples of all system features and an enumeration of all the specific requirements associated with these features")[1] and the nonfunctional requirements ("these aspects include system performance, costs, and such general system characteristics as reliability, security, and portability. The non-functional requirements also address aspects of the system development process and operational personnel").[2]

According to the Division of Library and Information Services statewide plan titled *Gateway to Information through Florida Libraries, 2003-2007,* "There was general recognition that continuing education (CE) at all levels of the organization, at all types of libraries, and with multiple partners, will be essential over the next five years."[3] In order to fulfill this essential need and to support the plan's goal, "librarians are well positioned for leadership in the twenty-first century."[4]

The statewide plan goes on to state that "Cooperatives have played and will continue to play an important, indeed central, continuing education role."[5] In direct response to this need, SEFLIN, the largest multitype library consortium in Florida, serving 26 libraries in 350 service locations and with more than 3,000 library staff has identified that thousands of Southeast Florida library staff require improved knowledge, skills, and proficiencies in basic and advanced computer applications, management, library services, and leadership. As stated in Goal 3, Outcome 2.1 of the *Gateway to Information through Florida Libraries Outcomes Plan, 2003-2007,* SEFLIN plans to continue to serve as a partner with the Division of Library and Information Services to "Partner with libraries and multitype library cooperatives to develop leadership program" and Outcome 2.2—"Work with multitype library cooperatives to coordinate training for library staff."

Library staff must work and be successful in rapidly changing environments. To be successful, library staff must be able to take full advantage of the wealth of education and training delivered through a variety of technology-based methods. SEFLIN's unequivocal response to this critical need has been to effectively and efficiently plan, implement, and evaluate the *CLP* with its aim to provide improved library staff knowledge and skills.

The goal of *CLP* is to create and sustain a national model that can be replicated in libraries, regardless of size or location. Through the concept of a blended learning program, libraries can review the *CLP* and create a menu of learning opportunities wherein selected training methods may be employed based upon library size, budget, technology available, and willingness of participants to become engaged in the program.

The SEFLIN *CLP* supports library staff being trained to be successful in twenty-first-century libraries. To that end, the *CLP* includes three active components:

1. The "blended learning" component supports the *CLP* by providing library staff with learning opportunities through a multitude of delivery mechanisms including instructor-led, Web-based, streaming media and video, and satellite teleconferences. The *CLP* has demonstrated an innovative technology-based continuing education and training program for library staff by providing an accessible and flexible program of hands-on learning. The "blended learning" opportunity for library staff offers a full program of hundreds of courses delivered live and online, available seven days a week, twenty-four hours a day.

All training in the blended learning opportunities component of the *CLP* is based on needs identified in SEFLIN's "Needs Assessment" surveys conducted by SEFLIN annually, and followed up with evaluation surveys, focus groups, and formal discussions held during each subsequent year of the *CLP*. The results of these surveys and other survey methods have demonstrated the value of the program in improving library services through enhancing staff skills and ensuring a flow of detailed informational data supporting the *CLP*. In the most recent data collected, *85 percent of the respondents reported engagement in the CLP for the purposes of career advancement or professional enhancement.*

In seeking additional methods for library staff to access courses, workshops, and tutorial offerings, SEFLIN has developed a fully realized continuous education program consisting of a number of blended learning tools, many delivered through technology. Programs offered in the *CLP* take into account the individual learning styles of employees, the limitations of library training budgets, challenges of managing time away from the workplace, and the large geographic area occupied by member libraries.

The concept behind the SEFLIN blended learning model is to create a learning program, format it into modules, and provide the best medium to deliver those modules to the learner. SEFLIN has progressed since the program began in 2000, and today the various media employed include the following:

Traditional instructor-led classroom in training lab settings and instructor-led technology-assisted formats (the presenter uses PowerPoint or Internet support).

Performance support tools (more than 1,000 of the most popular information technology reference books available online to all staff).

Web-based training (technology training and university level training on library issues).

Video teletraining (VHS videos of previously presented workshops and seminars).

Teleconferences (satellite-delivered workshops and seminars on library issues presented by professionals in the field).

2. The second component of the *CLP* is active participation by library staff in a regional professional conference. Travel to national conferences for many library staff members is often out of the question. Only a very small number of Southeast Florida library staff is able to participate in state and national conferences owing to the expense of registration and travel costs. A high quality regional professional conference is an essential continuing education opportunity for library staff.

Professional library conferences offer excellent continuing education programs providing library staff with numerous learning opportunities during a single day. Therefore, under the *CLP,* SEFLIN plans, implements, and evaluates a professional conference of interest to library staff working in SEFLIN member libraries. The goal of this conference is to provide a regional conference emphasizing national issues of local importance to participants. The theme of this regional conference ranges from technology to reference to library support staff issues to international library issues that affect libraries throughout Southeast Florida. This daylong event offers 160-200 library staff currently working in libraries in the region, the opportunity to attend a series of workshops, lectures, demonstrations, hands-on review of new products and services, and visit an exhibits area. It serves as another invaluable deliverable to the library learner.

The target outcomes of an annual SEFLIN-sponsored regional conference on e-reference for example would be:

> To support librarians' understanding of new technologies.
> To increase librarians' knowledge of technology used in libraries to better serve and train the public.
> To provide a venue where professionals can network, and thus better communicate with each other on technology issues.
> To better cooperate with each other in a partnering environment within a multitype library consortium where technology is a vital issue.

3. The third component of the *CLP* is to provide a leadership institute that supports the *Gateway to Information through Florida Libraries'* plan to ensure that "librarians are well positioned for leadership in the twenty-first century." SEFLIN has a history of presenting successful regional institutes for middle managers and senior leaders through previous institutes, held in 2000 and 2002. SEFLIN annually plans, implements, and evaluates an *Institute for Library Leaders.* The goal of such an institute is to enhance the leadership knowledge and skills of 30-40 professional librarians working in middle management and senior leadership positions in SEFLIN member libraries. Participation in the two-day *Institute* provides participants an opportunity to be better prepared to contribute to the vitality, growth, and success of the library profession.

The training sessions focus on developing an understanding of leadership. Participants have the opportunity to explore management issues associated with the rapidly changing environment that libraries find themselves in. An intensive learning community will be established through which individuals and groups can discover and explore insights about themselves and about the organizations and groups they work with.

Competencies gained or enhanced by this *Institute* include

- awareness of self as a leader and manager
- ability to work effectively in groups

- ability to communicate effectively
- ability to creatively solve problems
- awareness of personal communication and leadership style
- knowledge of influencing skills
- understanding of the dynamics of the changing environment.

An additional intention and focus of the *Institute for Library Leaders* is to refresh and renew participants by encouraging the sharing of insights, personal reflection, and having fun. The *Institute* includes lectures as well as experiential learning exercises.

Three Components Leading to the CLP Web Site

Through focus groups, committee discussions, and board meetings, it became apparent that there was a need for a *CLP* Web site where all of the lifelong learning components of the *CLP* may be viewed, retrieved, and utilized in a single accessible location. As a response, SEFLIN created the *CLP* Web site. This Web site has been built into the very successful MyLibraryService.org Web site as a component of the "Services for Libraries and Library Staff" section of that site.

The Web site provides tools to help members explore the learning needs of their organizations as well as their own learning needs. The *CLP* Web site helps individuals create their own learning journeys and the best ways to meet their needs. The SEFLIN *CLP* assists members in finding a variety of resources. Their choices depend on content, learning style, available technology, time, and funding. The SEFLIN *Community of Learning* is organized so that individuals can find a variety of learning resources easily at one site.

The SEFLIN *CLP* Web site was organized so that individuals could find a variety of learning resources easily at one site. The Web site provides various approaches to the concept of lifelong learning. We ask users to begin with the consideration of individual courses, workshops, and tutorials, or groupings of these offerings in the form of "training tracks." Wherever possible, *CLP* offerings should be linked to the library's "core competencies" for library staff. Core competencies have been defined as, "skills present or creatable upon which the organization bases its operations and services and from which it creates its preferred future. Upon careful analysis, core competencies serve to *synthesize* one's skills and knowledge, and *define* one's performance requirements."

As the Web site evolves into an even greater and more powerful tool for staff working in SEFLIN member libraries, there will be further enhancements necessary to support new applications built for the site. Also, in working with the Web developers for the Web site, SEFLIN is able to create within the application, stand-alone modules, such as a calendaring function that can be replicated in future projects and/or for other libraries.

The *CLP* Web site has been operational since January 2004 and hundreds of staff working in SEFLIN member libraries have registered to participate in its courses, workshops, tutorials, and informational offerings. The Web site may be viewed at http://www.scflin.org/clp/index.cfm?

Conducting a Manager's Survey on Education and Training of Library Learners

Visible and sustainable support from library managers and administrators is critical for a library learner to succeed in a climate of continuous change. It is imperative that the training and development of library staff be viewed as a kind of long-term and continuous *human capital improvement plan.* Encouragement in the form of a comprehensible internal mechanism of processes and procedures is established and maintained to nourish the program. Also, if library managers and administrators themselves demonstrate a level of fluidity and flexibility and become active participants in the program, there is greater likelihood of success. This is a challenging task. It requires managers to

> Educate (staff) on the (learning) community and the value it brings to their job and the (library).
> Define learning parameters by setting specific learning plans that provide each associate with specific time to learn, goals for each learning time, and rewards for accomplishing defined goals.
> Coach and follow up on each associate's learning plan; ensuring that each learner is achieving the plans set in learning plans and following through with defined consequences for non-performance.

Recognize and reward each associate's accomplishments through recognition and motivational rewards.

Support and manage ongoing integration of topics and techniques learned into the (staff's) daily work.[6]

Quite simply, most library managers "want assurance that the investment in training has a positive impact on the organization. They are not asking for astronomical return on investment. They are not asking for a 100-page research report. They simply want to know that the training organization has control over its costs and an eye to the bottom line."[7] Make no mistake about it, those who suggest that there is no bottom line in libraries have never managed a budget that, in some libraries, can be as complicated as that found in any corporate CFO's office. Therefore, it is vital that libraries justify training dollars, as they must any other line item, and have the data to support their justification. Frequent target surveys and questionnaires provide libraries with those tools.

Prior to employing those tools, however, the library must ascertain how to measure the success of those dollars spent on staff training. Typically, there are two types of costs: *direct,* which are defined as costs that can be specifically identified with a particular project or program, and *indirect,* which are defined as costs that are incurred by an organization for common or joint objectives and that, therefore, cannot be identified specifically with a particular project or program. Staff training can be applied against both direct and indirect costs. Let us take a look at what the library's expected outcomes seeks to gain by providing continuous training to its staff.

Good training aligns the varying aspects of a business and gives its employees the skills and capabilities required to bring about a change and its benefits. To maximize the benefits of training expenditures, a customized program should take into account the objectives of a change project, the people involved and their needs, and relevant time frames. Content rather than the method of delivery should be the top focus . . . Tom O'Toole of Beechworth Bakery in Canberra, Australia, when asked what happens if you train your people and they leave, answered, "What happens if you don't train them and they stay?" In order to respond to this question, a library manager's survey was developed, planned, and implemented.

One of the key ingredients in planning the *CLP* Web site was to understand the needs of the managers and their expectations regarding staff engagement in the *CLP*. To this end, a survey was designed to accomplish this information-gathering process as well as to fulfill one of the stated goals of the SEFLIN three-year strategic plan wherein library managers would be surveyed to understand the learning environment for staff working in their libraries and to highlight the strengths and weaknesses of the various levels of support. The template for this survey, entitled, "Training and Development Programs Assessment Survey for Managers" was designed by the Jack Phillips Center for Research. The results of this survey are available at http://www.seflin.org/clp/index.cfm?fuseaction=pages.TA Assessment Survey.

The survey was administered to the training administrators who serve as the information liaisons between the SEFLIN *CLP* and the staff working in their libraries. In order to review the training climate in each library, which, more often than not, determines the success or failure of any staff training program, this survey was designed to reveal specific strengths and weaknesses of the training support infrastructure, both practically and philosophically within each respondent's library. With this intent, this survey is to serve as a tool with which to perform an overall "environmental scan" of each library's training conditions to assist SEFLIN in providing a future *CLP* framework that is properly aligned with the needs of its member libraries. There was an overall response from eighteen of twenty-six libraries surveyed, a 69 percent response.

Scalability

Although SEFLIN planned its education and training program for a large consortium, this program is scalable to smaller library systems or even individual libraries. The scalability of a blended learning program is evident in its affordability. This program provides a menu-driven approach that can offer staff a variety of training tools. It is an approach that presents flexibility for libraries, which can add or subtract courses from the training menu, creating an individually designed learning program model. This is different from a traditional training program that solely relies on either permanent staff or hires presenters to train a group of staff in a specific area.

Sustainability

SEFLIN has steadily maintained that 5 percent of an annual salary budget line is the benchmark figure that should be used to support a modern library's training and development needs. As libraries experience formidable challenges in staffing, there must be some premium that libraries offer their staff, so to retain skilled employees.

An extended program of continuous staff training is critical to the success of a library in providing quality services to users. SEFLIN member libraries, whose staff have benefited from the LSTA-funded *Technology Training Program for Southeast Florida Library Staff,* and now the *CLP,* are recognizing the essential importance of training in improving staff performance and to recruiting and retaining staff. In some cases, the continuous training and development of library staff is being supported with local library funds. However, regional, state, and national support for training of library staff is indispensable considering the overwhelming number of library staff needing all types of training and the high rate of technological change.

The SEFLIN vision for a properly sustainable level of financial support lay in the understanding by the administrations of its member libraries of the extraordinary value of continuous training. SEFLIN will continue to emphasize the importance of continuous training to its member libraries and will provide significant information regarding usage statistics and measurable outcomes in order to highlight the success of training in advancing the development of library staff and services. As implied in the statewide plan, *Gateway to Information through Florida Libraries,* financial support for a successful twenty-first-century continuing education and training program must be a shared responsibility between local libraries, regional cooperatives, and the Division of Library and Information Services. SEFLIN member libraries have demonstrated impressive matching support for the *CLP.* More than $380,000 in local equivalent staff time has been provided through library staff participation in *CLP* courses, workshops, and tutorials. SEFLIN has demonstrated and will continue to seek partnerships with its member libraries and the Division of Library and Information Services, as stated in Goal 3, Outcome 2.1 of the *Gateway to Information through Florida Libraries Outcomes Plan, 2003-2007*—"Partner with libraries and multitype library cooperatives to develop leadership program"—and Outcome 2.2—"Work with multi-type library cooperatives to coordinate training for library staff to support a sustainable continuing education and training program for Southeast Florida library staff."

SEFLIN member libraries currently employ more than 3,000 staff. The contributions by SEFLIN members may also be described in terms of the cost to SEFLIN member libraries in staff compensation for staff participating in SEFLIN sponsored continuing education and training. For example, in FY2002/2003, 2,582 library staff attended SEFLIN continuing education and training events. The local library "cost" or "match" for this continuing education and training program is valued at approximately $387,300 in local library salary/benefits (2,582 staff × $150 a day for salary/benefits).

In an article titled, "Cooperative Library Services in Southeast Florida: A Staff Perspective" written by Maris Hayashi, the benefits of this blended learning program for Southeast Florida library staff may be summarized as follows: "Collaborative relationships between library cooperatives and member libraries exist primarily to benefit library patrons and community users. Important relationships between cooperatives and their members' employees also exist, yet this aspect is rarely identified and discussed. Cooperatives provide the resources and services to staff that are necessary for the establishment and continuance of lifelong learning. Staff take the skills and knowledge they acquire and learn, and put them to use when providing high quality service to their library patrons."[8]

Chapter 7

Teaching and Measuring Information Literacy Training

The Challenge—Librarians Must Be Trained
to Teach Information Literacy to Students
in Collaboration with Educators

The American Library Association Presidential Committee on Information Literacy has indicated that "No other change in American society has offered greater challenges than the emergence of the Information Age."[1] In order to support this assertion, there clearly must be a mechanism in place to support the creation and implementation of information literacy education. The report goes on to define information literacy as follows: "Information Literacy is a set of abilities requiring individuals to 'recognize when information is needed and have the ability to locate, evaluate, and use effectively the needed information.'"[2] In order to achieve success in the teaching and learning or information literacy strategies, librarians must receive comprehensive training in the proper manner in which to provide this set of tools to students. The success of this training can be strengthened through a collaborative effort between librarians and educators.

This report and standard practice since the report was written has placed librarians squarely in the forefront of developing and implementing information literacy training for students. Increasingly, however, librarians are collaborating with faculty on a much larger scale in order to create information literacy training that is adaptable to all. The committee examined the environment during the late 1980s and examined the issues facing students, educators, and librarians. Their

The Challenges to Library Learning: Solutions for Librarians

goal was to recommend a number of long-term, workable solutions to what was then, as now, viewed as a growing national issue. Since that report was published, there have been innumerable efforts on behalf of librarians and educators to address the issue and develop workable solutions.

Author Diane Zabel reminds readers that the issue has been discussed over the course of nearly three decades. Zabel informs us that "[t]he volume of publishing related to information literacy and library instruction is staggering."[3] By indicating that there is equal validity in both of these informational deliverables, it is clear that librarians have an extremely important role to play in developing information literacy programs in an academic setting.

In all three articles, the reader will find references to information literacy as a priority for the concept of "lifelong learning." In a peer-reviewed article written by Thomas P. Mackey and Trudi E. Jacobson, the ALA Report is referenced specifically. In the article, the authors indicate that "The American Library Association's Presidential Committee on Information Literacy (1989) created an expansive framework for understanding IL as a process of 'lifelong learning'."[4] Thus, the argument for information literacy education serving as more than a single course of instruction is supported by the concept of lifelong learning. For years, library instruction served as a baseline training model to teach the basics of information literacy concepts to students. However, in the past several years, the library instruction model has developed into a comprehensive and continuous information literacy learning model because librarians and educators have come to agree that skills gained through "lifelong learning" are those that students take along with them into the "real world" environment.

That being the case, the ALA Committee Report goes on to take a particularly egalitarian view of information literacy. By linking information literacy instruction to one's economic position in society, the report highlights the consequences for many in society should they not receive adequate information literacy instruction indicating that "[m]inority and at-risk students, illiterate adults, people with English as a second language, and economically disadvantaged people are among those most likely to lack access to the information that can improve their situations."[5] Likewise, author Christine Bruce also suggests that information literacy has its potentially negative economic effects should it not be made available to specific individuals when she writes, "IL is generally seen as pivotal to the pursuit of lifelong learning, and central to achieving both personal empowerment and economic development."[6]

Finally, in the third article reviewed for this essay, Diane Zabel tackles the issue from the partnership aspect wherein she counsels that librarians and faculty collaborate to create information literacy instruction that is practical and noninvasive. Even she indicates an economic impact of such instruction when she writes about the issue of students, who are already having a difficult time paying for higher education tuition and fees, having to pay additional fees to complete a "credit course" in information literacy when she writes, "There is likely to be increased backlash over the spiraling cost of higher education"[7]

Zabel concentrates less on the economic impact of information literacy instruction and more on the importance of the collaboration between faculty and librarians in developing and implementing information literacy education in the education environment. Likewise, the ALA Presidential Committee concludes its report with a number of recommendations, one of which indicates, "A portion of the practicum or teaching experience of beginning teachers should be spent with library media specialists."[8] The thrust of this collaboration is also at the heart of the article by Mackey and Jacobson where they examine the concept of "library as classroom." This model places the librarians in the position of teachers and links them squarely with the faculty, thus creating the building blocks for this collaboration or "teaching alliances."

All the articles reviewed examine the need for continuous and highly developed information literacy education programs. While the economic impacts of not doing so are discussed, and the concept of "technology literacy" is reported by Christine Bruce as a component of information literacy as a whole, there is more than enough evidence in all these articles to support the concept of information literacy education as necessary to lifelong learning. Information literacy education has, in many ways, changed the nature of work librarians do and this collaborative effort with faculty will continue to bring the two professions together. Relevant continuous collaboration between librarians and educators will continue to produce the most successful programs.

For years, there was an ongoing discussion between the faculty and librarians regarding the "ownership" and "control" of information resources. It appeared that this was less necessary when the Internet made its resources available to all. It appeared that librarians would be needed less, and there would be an even greater disconnect between librarians and faculty. In truth, however, librarians are needed more now than ever because of this explosion of resources. Librarians serve as the gatekeepers to wending one's way through the maze of information resources. This change has required greater collaboration with faculty and on many campuses that collaboration has led to a very different model of library, the Learning Commons, a model wherein it is a place where the concept of "one-stop shopping" and information for all is offered.

The Learning Commons brings with it a very different model of service. It is a model wherein the role of librarian is even closer to that of the faculty because there is a considerable "teaching" component inherent in it. This model will undoubtedly, and is already, changing the manner by which college campus librarians work, but it will also support greater collaboration between the librarians and the faculty through a shared process.

After all, in order teach information literacy, the librarian must attend continuous education workshops, seminars, courses, and the like on the latest techniques, not only in teaching this skill, but also in being able to refer to the latest research in the field for the most effective resources to accomplish this mission.

In 2001, the Central Florida Library Cooperative's (Training) Project provided training throughout the eleven county region of Brevard, Flagler, Indian River, Lake, Okeechobee, Orange, Osceola, Seminole, St. Lucie, Sumter, and Volusia. The cooperative looked at the change in library staff's knowledge of technology and their increase in ability to serve library patrons. They surveyed participants, asking questions (regarding) the changes that occurred due to the training. Over 80 percent of respondents indicated increase in knowledge of specific technology and ability to provide assistance to patrons. This information got to the change in knowledge, skills, behavior, or condition of participants with little more effort than gathering information such as number of participants and comfort of the chairs.

How Can Librarians Measure the Success of Our Teaching?

One of the difficulties in measuring the success of teaching information literacy is how far can measurement go to attain the information regarding the success that training has had on library staff? Can this challenge be overcome with the proper approach to outcomes measurement?

According to Calhoun Wick and Roy Pollock of the Fort Hill Company in Wilmington, Delaware, we have entered a rather schizophrenic period for the in-depth measurement of the effect that library learning has on the patrons it serves since it now appears that "traditional measures of reaction—number of courses taught and participant counts—are no longer sufficient. More and more, training budgets are linked to learning analytics and outcomes assessment."[9]

Wick and Pollack also write, "We [trainers] are not in the business of providing classes, learning tools, or even the learning itself. We are in the business of facilitating improved business performance."[10] If this is the case, then training the staff has gone from providing chunks or knowledge, or just-in-time, or anywhere-anytime information to them in any one of a number of different learning methods, not to increase their own learning, skills and/or knowledge, but simply to provide a better product (in the case of libraries, information is that product) in the most fastidious and comprehensive manner possible.

We have gone from training staff to providing a service to allow the organization to serve its public in a more effective manner. So, does this philosophy get at the crux of how the success of the service delivery to the public has been successful in their lives? If it does, then, the shift in training philosophy as an effective delivery tool has worked, but, still, as an effective results tool, has it been an equal success?

Is it possible to employ the standard use of outcomes measurement in order to arrive at the answers to these questions? Traditionally,

> outcome-based evaluation may be defined as a systematic way to assess the extent to which a program has achieved its intended results (and poses the following overall questions):
>
> How has my program made a difference?
> How are the lives of the program participants better as a result of my program?"[11]

Moreover, one must be fully acquainted with the steps in the process of creating an outcome-based evaluation measurement process for properly creating, analyzing, and reporting on the results of the program.

The following may serve as a basic set of procedures to follow and work to be accomplished in order to arrive at desired results-sets:

> Establish overall evaluation goals for a context (i.e., purpose)
> Identify key dimensions to the context that inform evaluation design
> Identify and secure resources needed to conduct evaluation
> Develop evaluation plan including timeline
> Design draft evaluation instruments
> Pre-test draft evaluation instruments
> Finalize draft evaluation instruments
> Collect data
> Code data
> Analyze data
> Confirm data analysis with intercoder reliability testing and/or member checking where appropriate
> Write up findings
> Incorporate your findings on outcomes in reports for different audiences, newsletters, public presentations, and so on.[12]

> To successfully compete for public or private funds, libraries must develop evaluation practices that provide a compelling picture of the impact of their services. Outcome-based evaluation is an effective way to tell the stories and convey the impact that will convince funders and other stakeholders that libraries make a difference. It is also a planning tool that can help libraries increase their effectiveness in achieving results. Outcome-Based Evaluation (OBE) is a systematic method of assessing the extent to which a program has achieved its intended result.[13]

Perhaps one rather obvious, but nonetheless visible means of answering these questions is through outcomes-based evaluation. Can this measurement strategy be employed to assess if a library staff member attained knowledge through the library learning program that has led to patrons enjoying better lives because of the information imparted to them? Can results be as evident as, for example, the patron who has gained information provided by a well-trained library staffer on subjects such as

- Jobs
- Literacy
- Immigrant outreach
- Community referral information
- Higher education.

The best means in which to collect this information is, obviously, to ask. As long as patrons recognize that collecting follow-up data is not an intrusion into their private lives, and that the information, once collected, will be reported anonymously, there should be some success in this data collection process. Developing the proper data collection tool is the most significant aspect of design in order to collect the best data possible. In order to accomplish this task, libraries may wish to create the data collection tool in-house or, should resources be available, contract the work out to a consultant. Either way, the design of the tool is critical, and the targeted distribution is also critical. Therefore, significant planning and development must go into the design of the data collection tool to collect the results that will provide the most accurate follow-up data available. The outcomes sought must provide the library with the data that can be used to measure the success of teaching such an important skill as information literacy to the public. Data collected will prove critical in maintaining and sustaining this extremely important librarian-delivered teaching component.

While it is clear that OBE is not a panacea for measuring all library programs and services, it is a process that may be employed to measure the success of librarians teaching information literacy. Much of the measurement data will be more anecdotal than statistical and the library may wish to employ focus-groups, surveys, and one-to-one patron/librarian interviews to gather this data. Using the ACRL Information Literacy Competency Standards for Higher Education will dictate the parameters of the skills that need to be measured and will

indicate the expected outcomes and indicators of success defining the information literate patron. These are present as follows:
A person who is information literate is able to:

- *Determine* the extent of the information needed
- *Access* the needed information effectively and efficiently
- *Evaluate* information and its sources critically
- *Incorporate* selected information into one's knowledge base
- *Use* information effectively to accomplish a specific purpose
- *Understand* the economic, legal and social issues surrounding the use of information
- *Access* and use information ethically and legally.[14]

The solution for assessing these measures of success may indeed be outcomes-based evaluation. In assessing the skills of the patrons who have gone through the learning experience, librarians can ascertain whether or not their training program has benefited themselves as well as their patrons.

Appendix

PowerPoint Presentation
on Design and Implementation
of a Training Program for Library Staff

This PowerPoint presentation is based on material appearing in the author's previous works, published by The Haworth Press, Inc., *The Practical Library Manager* (2003) and *The Practical Library Trainer* (2004).

The Challenges to Library Learning: Solutions for Librarians

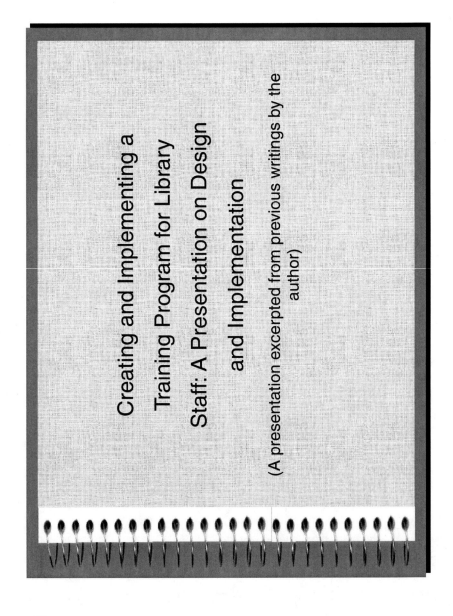

Creating and Implementing a Training Program for Library Staff: A Presentation on Design and Implementation

(A presentation excerpted from previous writings by the author)

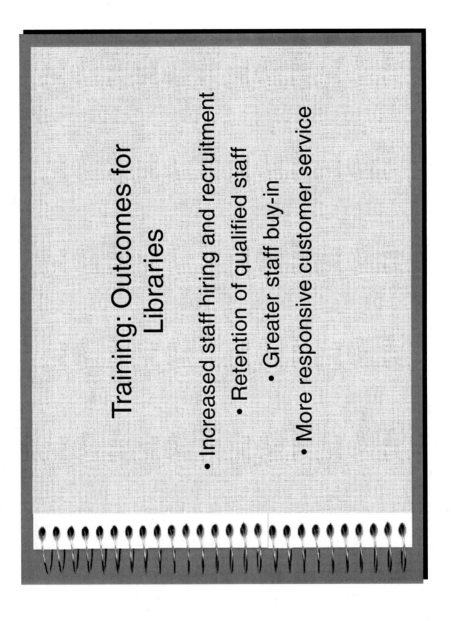

Training: Outcomes for Libraries

- Increased staff hiring and recruitment
- Retention of qualified staff
- Greater staff buy-in
- More responsive customer service

69

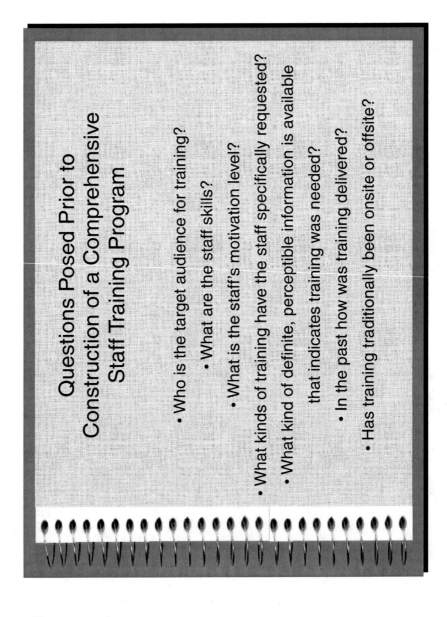

Questions Posed Prior to
Construction of a Comprehensive
Staff Training Program

• Who is the target audience for training?

• What are the staff skills?

• What is the staff's motivation level?

• What kinds of training have the staff specifically requested?

• What kind of definite, perceptible information is available
that indicates training was needed?

• In the past how was training delivered?

• Has training traditionally been onsite or offsite?

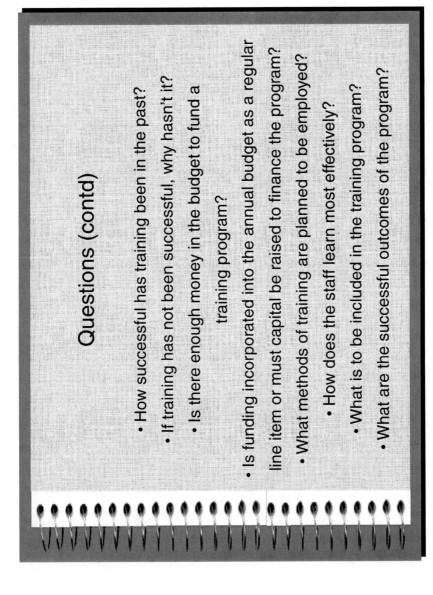

Questions (contd)

- How successful has training been in the past?
- If training has not been successful, why hasn't it?
- Is there enough money in the budget to fund a
  training program?
- Is funding incorporated into the annual budget as a regular
  line item or must capital be raised to finance the program?
- What methods of training are planned to be employed?
- How does the staff learn most effectively?
- What is to be included in the training program?
- What are the successful outcomes of the program?

Training Team Components

- The Survey Design Team
- The Instructional Design Team
- The Survey Analysis Team
- The Continuing Education and
  Training Team

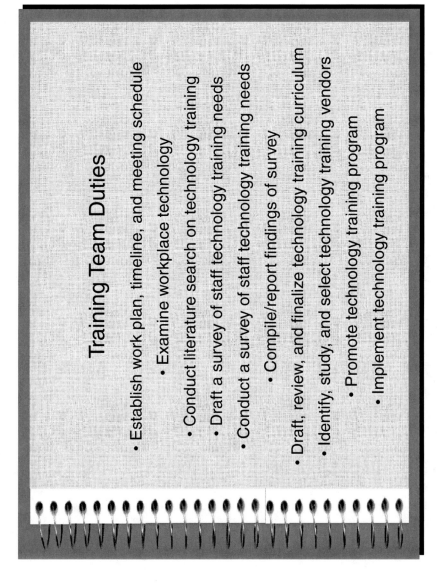

Training Team Duties

- Establish work plan, timeline, and meeting schedule
- Examine workplace technology
- Conduct literature search on technology training
- Draft a survey of staff technology training needs
- Conduct a survey of staff technology training needs
- Compile/report findings of survey
- Draft, review, and finalize technology training curriculum
- Identify, study, and select technology training vendors
- Promote technology training program
- Implement technology training program

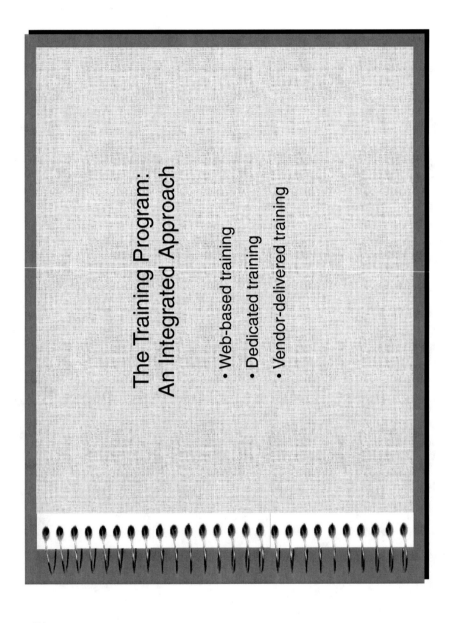

The Training Program:
An Integrated Approach

- Web-based training
- Dedicated training
- Vendor-delivered training

Web-Based Training: Vendor Deliverables

- Electronic "pre-" and "post" assessment evaluations
  - Comprehensive selection of courses
  - Courses accessible for reference purposes
- Courses must be downloadable for offline work
  - Courses may be taken any number of times
  - Courses must offer CE units
- Vendor must offer electronic reference books to support each course

Web-Based Training: Vendor Deliverables (contd)

- Vendor must offer electronic and live help desk
- Vendor must offer "instructor-led" and "self-study" courses
- Vendor must continue to offer new courses as these are developed
- Courseware must offer integration with "dedicated" and "voucher" courseware

Vendor-Delivered and Dedicated Training: Vendor Deliverables

- Classes synchronous with Web-based courseware
- Certified instructors
- Dedicated classes limited to 12 students
- Vouchers must be of use at any vendor location
- Courses must be available to replacement staff at discount
- Staff must be able to repeat a class at no additional cost
- Pre- and postassessments must be available to all students

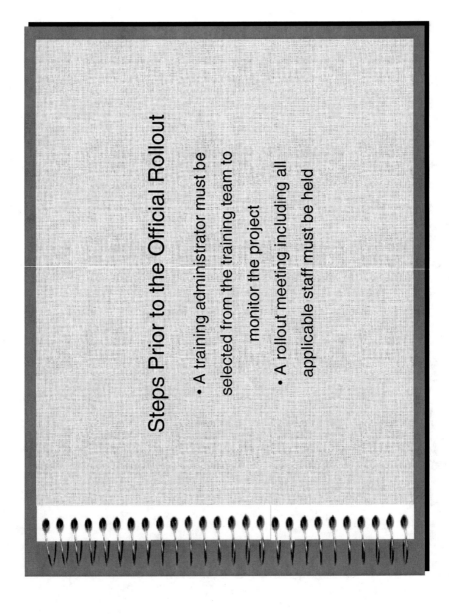

Steps Prior to the Official Rollout

- A training administrator must be selected from the training team to monitor the project

- A rollout meeting including all applicable staff must be held

Steps Prior to the Official Rollout

- Explain project plan to staff
  - Agree on goals
  - Explore vendor offerings
  - Explain staff's responsibilities
- Identify appropriate internal and external contacts
  - Distribute e-mail and phone list of students
  - Discuss maximum use of communication tools
- Identify and find solutions for any implementation barriers
  - Finalize timeline for implementation
  - Schedule site training and registration procedures

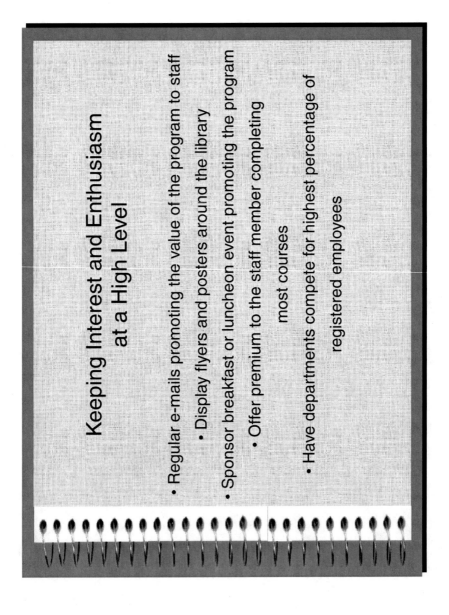

Keeping Interest and Enthusiasm
at a High Level

• Regular e-mails promoting the value of the program to staff

• Display flyers and posters around the library

• Sponsor breakfast or luncheon event promoting the program

• Offer premium to the staff member completing
most courses

• Have departments compete for highest percentage of
registered employees

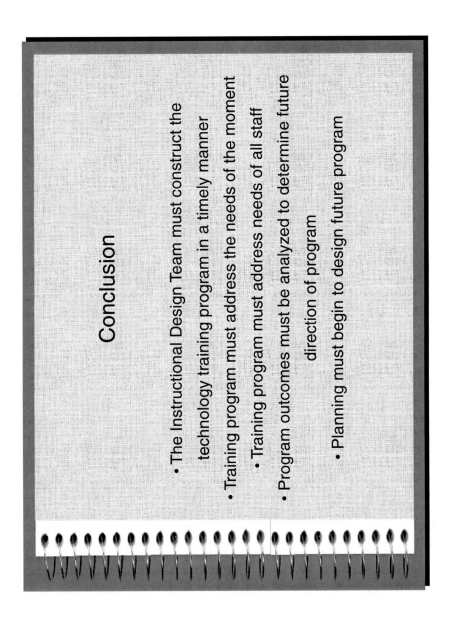

Conclusion

- The Instructional Design Team must construct the technology training program in a timely manner
- Training program must address the needs of the moment
- Training program must address needs of all staff
- Program outcomes must be analyzed to determine future direction of program
- Planning must begin to design future program

Notes

CHAPTER 1

1. Jim Loehr and Jack Groppel. (2004). *Full engagement*. Retrieved from the Web site, August 17, 2004, at http://www.clomedia.com/content/templates/clo_col_engagement.asp?articleid=375&zoneid=119.

2. The Virtual Teacher Center. Retrieved from the Web site, April 17, 2003, at http://www.virtualteachercentre.ca/welcome.asp.

3. Nic Paton. (2006). Make employee engagement your "hub," not an afterthought. Retrieved from the Web site, February 13, 2007, at http://www.management-issues.com/2006/8/24/research/make-employee-engagement-your-hub-not-an-after-thought.asp.

CHAPTER 2

1. D. Hewitt. (2005). The Boston Center for Adult Education. Retrieved from the Web site, December 29, 2005, at http://www.bcae.org/aboutframe.html.

2. Communities celebrate National Library Week, April 18-24, as public library visits near 1.2 billion. ALA Online. Retrieved from the Web site, December 30, 2005, at http://www.ala.org/Template.cfm?Section=News&template=/ContentManagement/ContentDisplay.cfm&ContentID=61206.

3. The Big Picture. OnlineLearning.net. Retrieved from the Web site, December 30, 2005, at http://www.onlinelearning.net/OLE/bigpicture.html?s=723.y040l435z.0930521c30.

4. V. Shea. (2004). *The Core Rules of Netiquette*. Retrieved from the Web site, September 30, 2005, at http://www.albion.com/netiquette/corerules.html.

5. Libraries and the enhancement of e-learning. Dublin, OH: OCLC. Retrieved from the Web site, May 31, 2004, at http://www5.oclc.org/downloads/community/elearning.pdf.

CHAPTER 3

1. Hal Macomber. (2004). Preparing your personal learning plan. Good2Great™ Associates. Retrieved from the Web site, May 19, 2004, at http://www.halmacomber.com/Preparing_Learning_Plan1.html.

2. Smart Goals. University of Victoria. Retrieved from the Web site, December 4, 2007, at http://www.coun.uvic.ca/learning/time-management/smartgoals.html.

CHAPTER 4

1. The Hay Group. (2004). Designing the accountable organization. White paper. Philadelphia, PA: Hay Group Headquarters, p. 9.

2. Substitute Librarian Sample 1. Montana State Library. Retrieved from the Web site, April 30, 2004, at http://msl.state.mt.us/ldd/Samples/PositionDescriptions/substlib1.html.

3. Claire Belilos. (2004). Cross-training as a motivational and problem-solving technique. *CHIC* Hospitality Consulting Services. Retrieved from the Web site, April 22, 2004, at http://www.easytraining.com/crosstrain.htm.

4. The Hay Group. (2004). Designing the accountable organization. White paper. Philadelphia, PA: Hay Group Headquarters, p. 3.

CHAPTER 5

1. Sophie Oberstein and Jan Alleman. (2003). *Beyond free coffee and donuts.* Alexandria, VA: ASTD.

2. Retrieved from the Web site, August 13, 2003, at http://ed.isu.edu/addie/.

3. Teresa Davenport. (2001, February). *Marketing training programs* (Info-line). Alexandria, VA: ASTD.

4. C. Shepard. (2003, November 20). How public libraries can pay for staff development {Msg 4}, Message posted to learnFF@lists.chilibsys.org.

5. Ibid.

6. See note 1 above.

7. Retrieved from the Web site, August 15, 2003, at http://www.astd.org/CMS/templates/index.html?template_id=1&articleid=26903.

8. See note 3 above.

CHAPTER 6

1. Requirements specification document outline. (2004). Retrieved from the Web site, February 2, 2004, at http://www.csc.calpoly.edu/~gfisher/classes/205/handouts/spec-doc-outline.html.

2. Ibid.

3. Gateway to Information through Florida Libraries: An Outcomes Plan. (2003-2007). Florida Department of State. Division of Library and Information Services, p. 18.

4. Ibid., p. 19.

5. Manager's Info. (2004). University of Denver. Retrieved from the Web site, March 15, 2004, at http://sp1.skillsoft.com/sp30060/custom/managers.htm.

6. Gene Salois. (2004). Case studies in the ROI of training. Retrieved from the Web site, April 16, 2004, at http://www.clomedia.com/content/anmviewer.asp?a=132&print=yes.

7. The key to effective change management. *Canberra Times* (Australia) (February 7, 2006), p. A27.

8. Maris L. Hayashi, "Cooperative Library Services in Southeast Florida: A Staff Perspective." *Resource Sharing and Information Networks: Innovations in Library Consortia, Systems, and Networks for Interlibrary Cooperation.* 18.12 (2005), pp. 61-71. Abstract.

CHAPTER 7

1. American Library Association. (1989). *Presidential Committee on Information Literacy: Final report.* Retrieved from the Web site, March 28, 2006, at http://www.ala.org/ala/acrl/acrlpubs/whitepapers/presidential.htm.

2. Ibid., p. 2.

3. D. Zabel. (2004, January). A reaction to "Information literacy and higher education." *Journal of Academic Librarianship* 30(1): 17-21.

4. T. Mackey and T. Jacobson. (2005, Fall). Information literacy: A collaborative endeavor. *College Teaching* 53(4): 140-144.

5. See note 1 above.

6. C. S. Bruce. (2003). *Information literacy as a catalyst for educational change: A background paper,* Retrieved from the Web site, March 28, 2006, at http://www.nclis.gov/libinter/infolitcomf&meet/papers/bruce-fullpaper.pdf.

7. See note 2 above.

8. See note 1 above.

9. C. Wick and R. Pollock. (2004, June). Making results visible. *T&D Magazine,* p. 47.

10. Ibid., p. 47.

11. Measuring program outcomes: Outcome-based evaluation for the 21st century librarian. (2004). Washington, DC: Institute of Museum and Library Services, p. 2.

12. Ibid.

13. Preparing for evaluation. (2004). School of information. University of Michigan. Retrieved from the Web site, October 1, 2004, at http://ibec.ischool.washington.edu/ibecCat.aspx?subCat=Outcome%20Toolkit&cat=Tools%20and%20Resources&tri=toolkitStep1c.

14. Definition of Information Literacy. (2001). Washington State Library. Retrieved from the Web site, November 28, 2007, at http://www.librarysmart.com/working/forlibraries/resource_pdfs/librarian_handouts/infolitdefinition.doc.

Selected Bibliography

Note: While the speed of technology dictates a complete overhaul of resources almost completely every eighteen months or less, some of the materials listed here may appear hopelessly out of date. However, they have been selected for their relevance to this book. The reader will kindly take note that some of the titles published prior to the turn of the century (2000) are listed here more for their pertinent historical value, and in some instances, their forecasting abilities rather than for their present-day significance.

Abbey, B. (Ed.). (2000). *Instructional and cognitive impacts of Web-based education.* Hershey, PA: Idea Group.

Aggarwal, A. (Ed.). (2000). *Web-based learning and teaching technologies: Opportunities and challenges.* Hershey, PA: Idea Group.

Alesso, H. P., & Smith, C. F. (2001). *The intelligent wireless web.* Indianapolis, IN: Addison Wesley Professional.

Alexander, L. (2000). *Education and training on the Internet: An essential source for students, teachers and education providers.* Plymouth: Internet Handbooks.

Anglin, G. J. (1999). *Critical issues in instructional technology* (Instructional Technology Series). Englewood, CO: Teacher Ideas Press.

Armstrong, S. (1995). *Telecommunications in the classroom* (Second edition). Eugene, OR: International Society for Technology in Education.

Ashby, W. R. (1956). *An introduction to cybernetics.* London: Chapman & Hall.

Bates, T. (1995). *Technology, open learning, and distance education.* London and New York: Routledge.

Bear, J., & Bear, M. (2002a). *Bears guide to earning degrees by distance learning.* Berkeley, CA: Ten Speed Press.

Bear, J., & Bear, M. (2002b). *College degrees by mail and Internet.* Berkeley, CA: Ten Speed Press.

Belanger, F., & Jordan, D. (1999). *Evaluation and implementation of distance learning: Technologies, tools and techniques.* Hershey, PA: Idea Group.

Berge, Z. L. (1994). *Computer-mediated communications and the online classroom* (Communication Series Communication Pedagogy and Practice Subseries). Cresskill, NJ: Hampton Press.

Berge, Z. L. (Ed.) (2000). *Sustaining distance training: Integrating learning technologies into the fabric of the enterprise.* San Francisco, CA: Jossey-Bass.

The Challenges to Library Learning: Solutions for Librarians

Berge, Z. L., & Collins, M. P. (Eds.). (1994a). *Computer-mediated communication and the online classroom (vol. 1)*. Cresskill, NJ: Hampton Press.

Berge, Z. L., & Collins, M. P. (Eds.). (1994b). *Computer-mediated communication and the online classroom (vol. 2)*. Cresskill, NJ: Hampton Press.

Berge, Z. L., & Collins, M. P. (Eds.). (1995). *Computer-mediated communication and the online classroom (vol. 3)*. Cresskill, NJ: Hampton Press.

Berge, Z. L., & Collins, M. P. (Eds.). (1997a). *Wired together: The online classroom in k-12: Perspectives and instructional design (vol. 1)*. Cresskill, NJ: Hampton Press.

Berge, Z. L., & Collins, M. P. (Eds.). (1997b). *Wired together: The online classroom in k-12: Case studies (vol. 2)*. Cresskill, NJ: Hampton Press.

Bonk, C. J., & King, K. S. (Eds.). (1998). *Electronic collaborators: Learner-centered technologies for literacy, apprenticeship, and discourse*. Mahwah, NJ: Erlbaum.

Branham, L. (2006). Manager to employee: Engage thyself. Retrieved from the Web site on December 6, 2006, at http://www.astd.org/NR/rdonlyres/6267344B-F4A0-449E-8B43-6DEECF80C71D/3091/Branhamemployeeengagement.pdf.

Braun, L. W., & Noah, C. (2002). *The Browsable classroom: An introduction to e-learning for librarians* (Neal-Schuman Netguide Series). New York: Neal-Schuman.

Browner, S. (2000). *Stephen Pulsford, and Richard Sears, literature and the Internet: A guide for students, teachers, and scholars*. London and New York: Garland.

Burge, E. J., & Haughey, M. (Eds.). (2002). *Using learning technologies*. London: Routledge.

Burgess, W. E. (Ed.) (2000). *The Oryx guide to distance learning: A comprehensive listing of electronic and other media-assisted courses*. Westport, CT: Oryx Press.

Campbell, L. (2002). *Mindful learning: 101 Proven strategies for student and teacher success*. Thousand Oaks, CA: Corwin Press.

Cantor (1992). *Delivering instruction to adult learners*. Toronto: Wall & Emerson.

Castro, C. M. (Ed.). (1998). *Education in the information age: What works and what doesn't*. Washington, DC: Inter-American Development Bank.

Chute, A. G., Thompson, M., & Hancock, B. (1998). *Handbook of distance learning*. New York: McGraw-Hill.

Clarke, Alan. (2000). *Designing computer-based learning materials*. London: Gower.

Cocking R. R., & Renninger, K. A. (Eds.). (1993). *The development and meaning of psychological distance*. Hillsdale, NJ: Lawrence Erlbaum Associates.

Collis, B. (1996). *Tele-learning in a digital world*. London: International Thomas Computer Press.

Collis, B., & Knezek G. (1997). *Teaching and learning in the digital age—research into practice with telecommunications in educational settings*. Eugene, OR: International Society for Technology in Education.

Collison, G., Elbaum, B., Haavind, S., & Tinker, R. (2000). *Facilitating online learning: Effective strategies for moderators*. Madison, WI: Atwood.

Connick, G. P. (Ed.). (1998). *The distance learner's guide*. Englewood Cliffs, NJ: Prentice Hall.

Cornell, R. A., & Murphy, K. (Eds.). (1995). *An international survey of distance education and teacher training: From smoke signals to satellite II.* Orlando, FL: University of Central Florida, and Paris: International Council for Educational Media.

Cotton, E. G. (1998). *The online classroom: Teaching with the Internet* (Second edition). Bloomington, IN: EDINFO Press.

Criscito, P. (2002). *Guide to distance learning: The practical alternative to standard classroom education* (Barrons Educational Series). Hauppauge, NY: Barron's Educational Series.

Cronin, M. J. (1996). *The Internet strategy handbook.* New York: McGraw-Hill.

Cummins, J., & Sayers, D. (1995). *Brave new schools: Challenging cultural literacy through global learning networks.* New York: St. Martin's Press.

Cyrs, T. E. (1997). *Teaching and learning at a distance: What it takes to effectively design, deliver, and evaluate programs.* San Francisco, CA: Jossey-Bass.

Cyrs, T. E. (1997). *Teaching at a distance with the merging technologies: An instructional systems approach.* Las Cruces, NM: New Mexico State University, Center for Educational Development.

Daniel, J. (1998) *Mega-universities and knowledge media: Technology strategies for higher education.* Sterling, VA: Stylus Publishing LLC.

Dean, G. J. (1994). *Designing instruction for adult learners.* Florida: Krieger.

Defining Outcome-Based Evaluation. (2003) School of Information. University of Michigan. Retrieved from the Web site on August 23, 2004, at http://ibec .ischool.washington.edu/ibecCat.aspx?subCat=Outcome percent20Toolkit&cat= Tools percent20and percent20Resources&tri=toolkitStep1a.

Dick, W., & Carey, L. (1996). *The systematic design of instruction* (Third edition). Glenview, IL: Scott Foresman.

Draves, W. A. (2002). *Teaching online* (Second edition). River Falls, WI: LERN Books.

Driscoll, M. M., & Alexander, L. (1998). *Web-based training: Using technology to design adult learning experiences.* San Francisco, CA: Jossey-Bass.

Duffy, J. P. (1997). *College online: How to take college courses without leaving home.* New York: John Wiley & Sons.

Duggleby, J. (2000). *How to be an online tutor.* Hampshire: Gower.

Duning, B., Van Kekerix, M., & Zaborowski, L. M. (1993). *Reaching learners through telecommunications.* San Francisco, CA: Jossey-Bass.

Durrance, J., & Fisher-Pettigrew, K. (2002). *How libraries and librarians help: Outcome-based evaluation toolkit.* Retrieved from the Web site, December 4, 2007, at http://ibec.ischool.washington.edu/ibecCat.aspx?subCat=Outcome%20 Toolkit&cat=Tools%20and%20Resources.

Dutton, W. H., & Loader, B. D. (2000). *Digital academe: The new media and institutions of higher education and learning.* London: Routledge.

Earnshaw, R., & Vince, J. (Eds.). (1997). *The Internet in 3D: Information, images, and interaction.* San Diego: Academic Press.

Eastmond D. V. (1995). *Alone but together: Adult distance study through computer conferencing.* New York: Hampton Press.

Ellis, A. L., Longmire, W. R., & Wagner, E. D. (1999). *Managing Web-based training.* Alexandria, VA: American Society for Training & Development.

Ely, D. P. (1996). *Trends in educational technology.* Syracuse University, NY: Informational Resources.

Evans, T., & Nation, D. (Eds.). (1996). *Opening education: Policies and practices from open and distance education.* New York: Routledge.

Fields, D. K., & Kolb, M. A. (2000). *Web development with JavaServer pages.* Greenwich, CT: Manning Publications Co.

Filho, W. L., & Tahir, T. (Eds.). (1998). *Distance education and environmental education.* New York: Peter Lang.

Finkelstein, M. J., Frances, C., Jewett, F. I., & Scholz, B. W. (Eds.). (2000). *Dollars, distance and online education.* Westport, CT: Oryx Press.

Fleming, M., & Levie, W.H. (1993). *Instructional message design* (Second edition). Englewood Cliffs, NJ: Educational Technology.

Florida Department of State, Division of Library and Information Services. (2000). *Workbook: Outcome measurement of library programs.* http://dlis.dos.state .fl.us/bld/Research_Office/OutcomeEvalWkbk.doc.

Fornal, P., & Sanchez, D. (2005) Employee engagement and organizational performance: How do you know your employees are engaged? http://www.astd.org/ NR/rdonlyres/196D5C24-5FB5-4E73-A11B-658E8BDA28D2/6894/Employee RetentionandEngagement.pdf.

Forsyth, F., Provenzo, Jr., Provenzo, E. F., & Forsyth (1999). *The Internet and the World Wide Web for preservice.* Boston: Allyn & Bacon.

Frazier, G., & Frazier, D. (1994). *Telecommunications and education: Surfing and the art of change.* Alexandra, VA: National School Boards Association.

Freeman, H., Routen, T., Patel, D., Ryan, S., & Scott, B. (1999). *The virtual university: The Internet and resource based learning* (The Open and Distance Learning Series). London: Kogan Page.

French, D., Hale, C., Johnson, C., & Farr, G. (Eds.). (1999). *Internet based learning: An introduction and framework for higher education and business.* Sterling, VA: Stylus.

Garrison, D. R., & Shale, D. (Eds.). (1990). *Education at a distance: From issues to practice.* Malabar, FL: Robert E. Krieger.

Gascoyne, R. J., & Ozcubucku, K. (1996). *The corporate Internet planning guide.* New York: Van Nostrand Reinhold.

Gayeski, D. (1998). *Designing and managing computer mediated instruction: An interactive toolkit.* Ithaca, NY: OmniCom Associates.

Gehris, D. O. (1997). *Using multimedia tools and applications on the Internet.* Belmont, CA: Wadsworth.

Giardina, M. (Ed) (1992). *Interactive multimedia environments.* Heidelberg: Springer-Verlag.

Gibson, C. C. (Ed.). (1998). *Distance learners in higher education.* Overland Park, KS: Atwood.

Gillis, L. (2000). *Quality standards for evaluating multimedia and online training.* Columbus, OH: McGraw-Hill.

Gilster, P. (1998). *Digital literacy.* New York: John Wiley & Sons.

Glavac, M. (1998). *The busy educator's guide to the World Wide Web.* NIMA Systems.

Grey, Duncan. (1999). *The Internet in school.* London: Cassell.

Hall, B. (1997). *Web-based training cookbook.* New York: Wiley.

Handler, M. G., & Dana, A. S. (1998). *Hypermedia as a student tool: A guide for teachers.* Englewood, CO: Libraries Unlimited.

Hanna, D. E., Glowacki-Dudka, M., & Conceicao-Runlee, C. (2000). *147 Practical tips for teaching online groups: Essentials of Web-based education.* Madison, WI: Atwood.

Hanson, D., Maushak, N., Schlosser, C., Anderson, M., Sorenson, C., & Simonson, M. (1997). *Distance education: Review of the literature* (Second edition). Washington, DC: Association for Educational Communications and Technology.

Harasim, L. (Ed.). (1990). *Online education: Perspectives on a new environment.* New York: Praeger.

Harasim, L., Hiltz, S. R., Teles, L., & Turoff, M. (1995). *Learning networks: A field guide to teaching and learning online.* Cambridge, MA: MIT Press.

Harmon, C. (1996). *Using the Internet, online services, and CD-ROMs for writing research and term papers.* New York: Neal-Schuman.

Harper, D., Hardy, J., & Murray, R. (1999). *Generation www.Y curriculum guide.* Eugene, OR: International Society for Technology in Education.

Harris, J. (1998). *Virtual architecture: Designing and directing curriculum based telecomputing.* Eugene, OR: International Society for Technology in Education.

Harrison, N. (1996). *Practical instructional design for open learning materials: A modular course covering open learning, computer-based training, multimedia.* New York: McGraw-Hill.

Harrison, N. (1998). *How to design self-directed and distance learning: A guide for creators of web-based training, computer-based training, and self-study materials.* New York: McGraw-Hill.

Harry, K. (1999). *Higher education through open and distance learning.* London: Routledge.

Harry, K., John, M., & Keegan, D. (Eds.). (1993). *Distance education: New perspectives.* London: Routledge.

Hartley, D. (2000). *On-demand learning: Training in the new millennium.* Amherst, MA: HRD Press.

Haughey, M., & Anderson, T. (1998). *Networked learning: The pedagogy of the Internet.* Toronto: McGraw-Hill.

Havelock, R. G., & Zlotolow, S. (1995). *The change agent's guide.* Englewood Cliffs, NJ: Educational Technology.

Hawkins, B. (Ed.). (1998). *The mirage of continuity: Reconfiguring academic information resources for the 21st century.* Washington, DC: Council on Library and Information Resources.

Hazemi, R., Hailes, S., & Wilbur, S. (Eds.). (1998). *The digital university: Reinventing the academy.* London: Springer-Verlag.

Head, A. J. (1999). *Design wise: A guide to evaluating the interface design of information resources.* Medford, NJ: Information Today.

Hegarty, M., Phelan, A., & Kilbride, L. (Eds.). (1998), *Classrooms for distance teaching and learning: A blueprint.* Leuven, Belgium: Leuven University Press.

Heide, A., & Stilborne, L. (1999). *The teacher's complete and easy guide to the Internet.* Buffalo, NY: Trifolium Books.

Heinich, R., Molenda, M., Russell, J., & Smaldino, S. (1996). *Instructional media and technologies for learning.* Upper Saddle River, NJ: Prentice Hall.

Heldman, R. (1993). *Future telecommunications information applications, services, and infrastructure.* Washington, DC: McGraw-Hill.

Hernon, P., & Dugan, R. E. (2002). *Action plan for outcomes assessment in your library.* Chicago, IL: American Library Association.

Hiltz, S. R. (1993). *The virtual classroom: A new option for learning via computer networking.* Norwood, NJ: Ablex.

Hiltz, S. R. (1994). *The virtual classroom: Learning without limits via computer networks.* Norwood, NJ: Ablex.

Hiltz, S. R., & Turoff, M. (1993). *The network nation: Human communication via computer.* Cambridge, MA: MIT Press.

Hixson, S., & Schrock, K. (1998). *Developing web pages for school and classroom authors: Beginner's handbook.* Westminster, CA: Teacher Created Resources.

Holmberg, B. (1995). *Theory and practice of distance education.* London: Routledge.

Horn, Claudia B. (2001). *Outcome-based evaluation for literacy programs.* Syracuse, NY: Literacy Volunteers of America.

Horton, S. (2000). *Web teaching guide: A practical approach to creating course Web sites.* New Haven, CT: Yale University Press.

Horton, W. K. (2000). *Designing Web-based training: How to teach anyone anything anywhere anytime.* New York: John Wiley & Sons.

Horton, William K. (2002). *Using e-learning.* Alexandria, VA: American Society for Training and Development.

Hudspeth, D. (1985). *Instructional telecommunications.* New York: Praeger.

Insinnia, E. (Ed.). (1999). *Educators take charge: Teaching in the Internet revolution.* Eugene, OR: International Society for Technology in Education.

Jacobson, R. E. (Ed.). (1999). *Information design.* Cambridge, MA: MIT Press.

Johnson, J. K. (1995). *Degree curricula in educational communications and technology: A descriptive directory 1995/with disk* (Fifth edition). Washington, DC: Association for Educational Communications and Technology.

Jonassen, D. H. (Ed.). (1996). *Handbook of research on educational communications and technology: A project of the association for educational communications and technology.* New York: MacMillan.

Jones, S. (2000). *The Internet for educators and homeschoolers.* Palm Springs, CA: ETC Publications.

Kafai, Y., & Resnick, M. (Eds.). (1996). *Constructionism in practice: Designing, thinking, and learning in a digital world.* Hillsdale, NJ: Lawrence Erlbaum Associates.

Katz, R. (Ed.). (1999) *Dancing with the devil: Information technology and the new competition in higher education.* San Francisco, CA: Jossey-Bass.

Kearsley, G. (2000). *Online education: Learning and teaching in cyberspace.* Belmont, CA: Wadsworth.

Keegan, D. (1996). *Foundations of distance education.* London: Routledge.

Keegan, D. (Ed.). (1993). *Theoretical principles of distance education.* London: Routledge.

Keith, H. (Ed.) (1999). *Higher education through open and distance learning.* London: Routledge.

Kelleher, K., & Cross, T. B. (1985). *Teleconferencing: Linking people together electronically.* Englewood Cliffs, NJ: Prentice Hall.

Kember, D. (1995). *Open learning courses for adults: A model of student progress.* Englewood Cliffs, NJ: Educational Technology.

Kemp, J. E., Morrison, G. R., & Ross, S. M. (1997). *Designing effective instruction.* New York: Merrill.

Khan, B. H. (Ed.). (1997). *Web-based instruction.* Englewood Cliffs, NJ: Educational Technology.

Khan, B. H. (Ed.). (2002). *Web-based training.* Englewood Cliffs, NJ: Educational Technology.

Kirkup, G., Jones, A., & Kirkwood, A. (1993). *Personal computers for distance education: The study of an educational innovation.* New York: St. Martin's Press.

Knott, T. (1994). *Planning and evaluating distance education: A guide to collaboration.* Memphis: Diphara.

Ko, S. S., Rossen, S., & Ko, S. (2000). *Teaching online: A practical guide.* Boston, MA: Houghton Mifflin.

Kommers, P. A. M., Grabinger, S., & Dunlap, J. C. (1996). *Hypermedia learning environments: Instructional design and integration.* Mahwah, NJ: Lawrence Erlbaum.

Kurz, R. A., Newland, B. G., Lieberman, S., & Jimenez, C. M. (1996). *Internet and the law: Legal fundamentals for the Internet user.* Rockville, MD: Government Institutes.

Lamb, A. C., & Johnson, L. (1995). *Cruisin' the information highway: Internet and the k-12 classroom.* Evansville, IN: Vision to Action.

Latchem, C., & Lockwood, C. (Eds.). (1998). *Staff development in open and flexible learning.* London: Routledge.

Lennon, J. A. (1997). *Hypermedia systems and applications: World wide web and beyond.* New York: Springer-Verlag.

Leshin, C. B. (1998). *Focus on curriculum integration through Internet adventures.* Englewood Cliffs, NJ: Prentice Hall.

Leshin, C. B., Pollock, J., & Reigeluth, C. M. (1992). *Instructional design strategies and tactics.* Englewood Cliffs, NJ: Educational Technology.

Lewis, R., & Whitlock, Q. (2003). *How to plan and manage an e-learning programme.* London: Gower.

Lockwood, F. (Ed.). (1995). *Open and distance learning today.* London: Routledge.

Lynch, M. M. (2002). *The online educator: A guide to creating the virtual classroom.* New York and London: Routledge.

Lynch, P. J., & Horton, S. (1999). *Web style guide: Basic design principles for creating web sites.* New Haven, CT: Yale University Press.

Maddux, C. D., & Milheim, W. D. (Eds.). (1992). *Distance education: A selected bibliography.* Englewood Cliffs, NJ: Educational Technology.

Maeroff, Gene. (2003). *A classroom of one: How online learning is changing our schools and colleges.* Houndmills, Basingstoke, Hampshire, England: Palgrave Macmillan.

Mantyla, K., & Gividen, J. R. (1997). *Distance learning: A step-by-step guide for trainers.* Washington, DC: CRC Press.

Marcus, A. (1992). *Graphic design for electronic documents and user interfaces.* New York: Addison-Wesley.

Margolis, P. E. (1999). *Random House personal computer dictionary* (Third edition). New York: Random House.

Martin, L. E. (1997). *The challenge of Internet literacy: The instruction-web convergence.* Binghamton, NY: Haworth Press.

Mason, R. (1998). *Globalising education: Trends and applications.* London: Routledge.

Mason, R., & Kaye, A. (Eds.). (1989). *Mindweave: Communication, computers, and distance education.* New York: Pergamon Press.

McCormack, C., & Jones, D. (1997). *Building a Web-based education system.* New York: John Wiley & Sons.

Miller, E. B. (1996). *The Internet resource directory for k-12 teachers and librarians 98/99 (Serial).* Englewood, CO: Libraries Unlimited.

Miller, S. (1998). *Searching the World Wide Web: An introductory curriculum for using search engines.* Eugene, OR: International Society for Technology in Education.

Minoli, D. (1996). *Distance learning technology and applications.* Cambridge, MA: Artech House.

Misanchuk, E. R., Schwier, R. A., & Boling, E. (2000). *Visual design for instructional multimedia.* University of Saskatchewan, Canada: U-Learn Extension Division.

Mood, T. A. (1995). *Distance education: An annotated bibliography.* Englewood, CO: Libraries Unlimited.

Moore, M. (Ed.). (1995). *Video-based telecommunications in distance education.* University Park, PA: American Center for the Study of Distance Education.

Moore, M. (Ed.). (1996). *Distance education for corporate and military training.* University Park, PA: American Center for the Study of Distance Education.

Moore, M. G., & Clark, G. C. (Eds.). (1989). *Readings in distance learning and instruction.* University Park, PA: American Center for the Study of Distance Education.

Moore, M. G., Cookson, P., & Donaldson, J. (Eds.). (1990). *Contemporary issues in American distance education.* New York: Pergamon Press.

Moore, M., & Kearsley, G. (1996). *Distance education: A systems view.* Belmont, CA: Wadsworth.

Moore, M. G., & Thompson, M. M. (1990). *The effects of distance learning: A summary of literature.* University Park, PA: American Center for the Study of Distance Education.

Moore, M. G., & Thompson, M. M. (1997). *The effects of distance learning* (ACSDE Research Monograph Series, vol. 15). University Park, PA: American Center for the Study of Distance Education.

Morgan, C., & O'Reilly, M. (1999). *Assessing open and distance learners.* United Kingdom: Kogan Page.

Moses, J. (1999). *The survey of distance learning programs in higher education 1999.* New York: Primary Research Group.

Moursund, D. (1997). *The future of information technology in education.* Eugene, OR: International Society for Technology in Education.

Mullet, K., & Sano, D. (1995). *Designing visual interfaces: communication oriented techniques.* Hillsdale, NJ: Prentice Hall.

Negroponte, N. (1996). *Being digital.* New York: Vintage Books.

Nielsen, J. (1996). *Multimedia and hypertext: The Internet and beyond.* San Diego, CA: Academic Press.

Nielsen, J. (1999). *Designing websites with authority: Secrets of an information architect.* Indianapolis, IN: New Riders.

O'Malley, C. (Ed.). (1995). *Computer supported collaborative learning.* New York: Springer-Verlag.

O'Reilly Associates. (Ed.). (1997). *The Harvard conference on the Internet and society.* Cambridge, MA: Harvard University Press.

Oblinger, D. G. (Ed.). (1997). *The learning revolution: The challenge of information technology in the academy.* Boston, MA: Anker.

Outcome-based evaluation (2003). Texas State Library and Archives Commission. Retrieved from the Web site, August 10, 2004, at http://www.tsl.state.tx.us/ld/pubs/obe/

Owen, T., & Ownston, R. (1998). *The learning highway: Smart students and the net.* Toronto: Key Porter Books.

Palloff, R. M., & Pratt, K. (1999). *Building learning communities in cyberspace: Effective strategies for the online classroom.* San Francisco, CA: Jossey-Bass.

Palloff, R. M., & Pratt, K. (2001). *The realities of online teaching.* San Francisco, CA: Jossey-Bass.

Palloff, R. M., & Pratt, K. (2003). *The virtual student: A profile and guide to working with online learners.* San Francisco, CA: Jossey-Bass.

Phillips, V., & Yager, C. (1999). *The best distance learning graduate schools 1999: Earning your degree without leaving home (serial).* Burlington, MA: Princeton Review.

Plomp, T., & Ely, D. P. (Eds.). (1996). *International encyclopedia of educational technology* (Second edition). New York: Pergamon Press.

Porter, L. R. (1997). *Creating the virtual classroom: Distance learning with the Internet.* New York: John Wiley & Sons.

Portway, P., & Lane, C. (1994). *Guide to teleconferencing and distance learning.* Cleveland, OH: Advanstar Communications.

Quarterman, J. S. (1990). *The matrix: Computer networks and conferencing systems worldwide.* Bedford, MA: Digital Press.

Rada, Roy (2001). *Understanding virtual universities.* Bristol: Intellect.

Reese, J. (1999). *Internet books for educators, parents and children.* Englewood, CO: Libraries Unlimited.

Rheingold, H. (1993). *The virtual community.* Reading, MA: Addison Wesley.

Roberts, N., Blakeslee, G., Brown, M., & Lenk, C. (1990). *Integrating telecommunications into education.* Englewood Cliffs, NJ: Prentice Hall.

Rogers, E. M. (1995). *Diffusion of innovations.* New York: The Free Press.

Romiszowski, A. J. (1981). *Designing instructional systems.* London: Kogan Page.

Rosenberg, M. J. (2001). *E-learning: Strategies for delivering knowledge in the digital age.* New York: McGraw-Hill.

Rosenfeld, L., & Morville, P. (1998). *Information architecture for the world wide web.* Cambridge: O'Reilly & Associates.

Rossman, M. H., & Rossman, M. E. (Eds.). (1995). *Facilitating distance education.* San Francisco, CA: Jossey-Bass.

Rouet, J., & Levonen, J. J. (Eds.). (1996). *Hypertext and cognition.* Mawhaw, NJ: Lawrence Erlbaum Associates.

Ryder, R. J., & Hughes, T. (1998). *Internet for educators.* Upper Saddle River, NJ: Prentice Hall.

Salmon, G. (2000). *E-moderating: The key to teaching and learning online* (Open and Distance Learning Series). London, England: Kogan Page.

Salmon, G. (2002). *E-tivities: The key to active online learning.* London, England: Kogan Page.

Sandholtz, J. H., Ringstaff, C., & Dwyer, D. C. (1997). *Teaching with technology: Creating student-centered classrooms.* New York: Teachers College Press.

Schank, R. C. (1997). *Virtual learning: A revolutionary approach to building a highly skilled workforce.* New York: McGraw-Hill.

Schreiber, D. A., & Berge, Z. L. (1998). *Distance training: How innovative organizations are using technology to maximize learning and meet business objectives.* San Francisco, CA: Jossey-Bass.

Schrum, L., & Berenfeld, B. (1997). *Teaching and learning in the information age: A guide to educational telecommunications.* Boston: Allyn & Bacon.

Seels, B., & Richey. (1994). *Instructional technology: The definition and domains of the field.* Washington, DC: Association for Educational Communications and Technology (AECT).

Serim, F., & Koch, M. (1996). *Netlearning: Why teachers use the Internet (Songline guides).* Cambridge: O'Reilly & Associates.

Sharp, V., Levine, M., & Sharp, R. (1998). *The best Web sites for teachers* (Second edition). Eugene, OR: International Society for Technology in Education.

Shea-Schultz, H., Fogarty, J., Shea, H., Shea, S. (2002). *Online learning today.* San Francisco, CA: Berrett-Koehler.

Shoemaker, C. J. (1998). *Leadership in continuing and distance education in higher education.* Boston, MA: Allyn & Bacon.

Simonson, M. R. (Ed.). (1999). *Teaching and learning at a distance: Foundations of distance education.* Upper Saddle River, NJ: Prentice Hall.

Smedinghoff, T. J. (Ed.). (1996). *Online law: The SPA's legal guide to doing business on the Internet.* Reading, MA: Addison-Wesley Developers Press.

Smith, P. L., & Ragan, T. J. (1999). *Instructional design.* New York: John Wiley & Sons.

Smith, W. L., & Lamb, A.C. (1998). *Virtual sandcastles.* Evansville, IN: Vision to Action.

Sproull, L., & Kiesler, S. (1991). *Connections: New ways of working in the networked organization.* Cambridge, MA: MIT Press.

Stammen, R. M. (1996). *Using multimedia for distance learning in adult, career, and vocational education.* Collingdale, PA: Diane Pub Co.

Steinaker, N. W., & Bell, M. R. (1979). *The experiential taxonomy: A new approach to teaching and learning.* New York: Academic Press.

Stevens, G. H., & Stevens, E. F. (1995). *Designing electronic performance support tools: Improving workplace performance with hypertext, hypermedia, and multimedia.* Englewood Cliffs, NJ: Educational Technology.

Tait, A., & Mills, R. (1999). *The convergence of distance and conventional education: Patterns of flexibility for the individual learner.* London: Routledge.

Tapscott, D. (1997). *Digital economy, promise and peril in the age of network intelligence.* New York: McGraw-Hill.

Teare, R., Davies, D., & Sandelands, E. (1999). *The virtual university: An action paradigm and process for workplace learning.* London: Cassell Academic.

Tennyson, R. D., Schott, F., & Seel, N. M. (1997). *Instructional design: International perspectives: Theory, research, and models.* Hillsdale, NJ: Lawrence Erlbaum Associates.

Thompson, M. M. (1996). *Internationalism in distance education: A vision for higher education.* State College, PA: American Center for the Study of Distance Education.

Thornburg, D. D. (1992). *Edutrends 2010: Restructuring, technology, and the future of education.* San Carlos, CA: Starsong.

Thornburg, D. D. (1994). *Education in the communication age.* San Carlos, CA: Starsong.

Thornburg, D. D. (1996). *Putting the web to work.* San Carlos, CA: Starsong.

Tiffin, J., & Rajasingham, L. (1995). *In search of the virtual class: Education in an information society.* London: Routledge.

Tyner, K. (1998). *Literacy in a digital world: Teaching and learning in the age of information.* Hillsdale, NJ: Lawrence Erlbaum Associates.

United Way of America. (1996). *Measuring program outcomes: A practical approach.* Alexandria, VA: United Way of America. (Portions are available online as of April 15, 2003.) http://national.unitedway.org/outcomes/library/pgmomres.cfm

Valauskas, E. J., & Ertel, M. (1996). *The Internet for teachers and school library media specialists: Today's applications, tomorrow's prospects.* New York: Neal-Schuman.

Van Merrienboer, Jeroen J. G. (1997). *Training complex cognitive skills: A four component instructional design model.* Englewood Cliffs, NJ: Educational Technology.

Vega, D. (1998). *Learning the Internet for kids: A voyage to Internet treasures.* Upper Saddle River, NJ: DDC.

Verduin, J. R., & Clark, T. A. (1991). *Distance education: The foundations of effective practice.* San Francisco, CA: Jossey-Bass.

Waggoner, M. D. (Ed.). (1992). *Empowering networks: Computer conferencing in education.* Englewood Cliffs, NJ: Educational Technology.

Wagner, E. D., & Koble, M. A. (Eds.). (1997). *Distance education symposium 3: Course design.* University Park, PA: American Center for the Study of Distance Education.

Warda, M. (1997). *How to register a U. S. copyright.* Clearwater, FL: Sphinx.

Welling, K. (1998). *Internet exploration: Activities and concepts.* Earlysville, VA: Computer Literacy Press.

Western Cooperative for Educational Telecommunications. (1998). *The distance learner's guide.* Upper Saddler River, NJ: Prentice Hall.

White, K. W., & Weight, B. H. (Eds.). (2000). *The online teaching guide.* Needham Height, MA: Allyn & Bacon.

Williams, M. L., Paprock, K., & Covington, B. (1998). *Distance learning: The essential guide.* Thousand Oaks, CA: Sage Publications.

Willis, B. (1994a). *Distance education: A practical guide.* Englewood Cliffs, NJ: Educational Technology.

Willis, B. (Ed.). (1994b). *Distance education: Strategies and tools.* Englewood Cliffs, NJ: Educational Technology.

Wilson, B.G. (1996). *Constructivist learning environments: Case studies in instructional design.* Englewood Cliffs, NJ: Educational Technology.

Wlodkowski, R. (1993). *Enhancing adult motivation to learn.* San Francisco, CA: Jossey-Bass.

Index